"*Mentoring Minutes* is a wonderful book that will be enormously helpful to programs and mentors alike. Through engaging quotes and upbeat messages, mentoring expert Robin Cox has found a way to deliver just the right balance of research and inspiration."

—JEAN RHODES
Frank L. Boyden Professor of Psychology, University of Massachusetts, Boston

"Cox's book gives endless practical advice to mentors alongside grounded mentoring theory. He carefully balances the primacy to build trust with the new research recommending a more intentional approach. The week by week format helpfully mirrors the mentoring journey and gives hope to the young people Cox shows such a belief in."

—MATTHEW BUTTON
Practice Manager, Big Brothers Big Sisters of New Zealand

"This book is an amazing resource for anyone working with a young person in a mentoring role—both in and outside of programs. A lifetime's worth of wisdom and insight has been collected and shared here. Robin has done a wonderful job of highlighting many of the intricacies of the art of mentoring and I hope this book encourages new mentors and fortifies those who are already supporting young people."

—MICHAEL GARRINGER
Director of Research and Evaluation, MENTOR: The National Mentoring Partnership

Mentoring Minutes

MENTORING MINUTES

Weekly Messages to Encourage Anyone Guiding Youth

Robin Cox

Foreword by
Susan G. Weinberger

RESOURCE *Publications* · Eugene, Oregon

MENTORING MINUTES
Weekly Messages to Encourage Anyone Guiding Youth

Copyright © 2020 Robin Cox. All rights reserved. Except for brief quotations in critical publications or reviews, no part of this book may be reproduced in any manner without prior written permission from the publisher. Write: Permissions, Wipf and Stock Publishers, 199 W. 8th Ave., Suite 3, Eugene, OR 97401.

Resource Publications
An Imprint of Wipf and Stock Publishers
199 W. 8th Ave., Suite 3
Eugene, OR 97401

www.wipfandstock.com

PAPERBACK ISBN: 978-1-7252-6945-3
HARDCOVER ISBN: 978-1-7252-6944-6
EBOOK ISBN: 978-1-7252-6946-0

Manufactured in the U.S.A.   JULY 31, 2020

ALSO BY ROBIN COX

The Mentoring Spirit of the Teacher—Inspiration, support and guidance for aspiring and practising teacher-mentors

Expanding the Spirit of Mentoring—Simple steps and fun activities for a flourishing peer mentor or peer support program

Nurturing the Spirit of Mentoring—50 fun activities for young people and for peer mentor training

Encouraging the Spirit of Mentoring—50 fun activities for the ongoing training of teacher-mentors, volunteer mentors, student leaders, peer mentors and youth workers

The Spirit of Mentoring—A manual for adult volunteers

Letter 2 a Teen—Becoming the Best I can Be

Making a Difference—The Teacher-Mentor, the Kids and the M.A.D Project

7 Key Qualities of Effective Teachers: Encouragement for Christian Educators

More information available at www.yess.co.nz

To my grandchildren Abigail and Charlotte:
with the hope that you will carry the spirit
of mentoring throughout your lives.
To all my trusted and valued mentors:
thank you for believing in me, often pushing me
out of my comfort zone,
always encouraging and inspiring me
to chase my dreams.

CONTENTS

Foreword by Susan G. Weinberger | xi
Preface: A Mentor's Dream | xiii

THE SPIRIT OF MENTORING—A CALL TO ACTION | 1

MENTORING MINUTES | 9

  Week 1: INTRODUCING MENTORING | 10

  Week 2: DIFFERENT MENTORING ROLES | 14

  Week 3: MENTORS AS ROLE MODELS | 19

  Week 4: YOUTH CULTURE | 23

  Week 5: CONNECT WITH YOUTH | 27

  Week 6: FEATURES OF ADOLESCENTS AGED BETWEEN ELEVEN AND NINETEEN | 32

  Week 7: MENTORING REFLECTIONS | 37

  Week 8: GOAL SETTING—A START | 42

  Week 9: UNDERSTAND RESILIENCY | 47

  Week 10: COMMUNICATION | 52

  Week 11: GOAL SETTING—THE PROCESS | 56

  Week 12: SELF-IMAGE | 61

  Week 13: LOOKING AT CONFLICT | 66

  Week 14: MENTORING REFLECTIONS | 70

  Week 15: ASSERTIVENESS | 75

  Week 16: COMMUNICATION INFLUENCES | 80

  Week 17: SIX STEP CONFLICT RESOLUTION PROCESS | 84

Week 18: FEATURES OF ADOLESCENTS AGED BETWEEN THIRTEEN AND FIFTEEN | 89

Week 19: DEALING WITH STRESS | 94

Week 20: CHALLENGING ISSUES | 99

Week 21: MENTORING REFLECTIONS | 104

Week 22: FATIGUE | 108

Week 23: ACHIEVE GOALS | 113

Week 24: LISTEN! LISTEN! | 117

Week 25: GENERAL ISSUES | 121

Week 26: RELATIONSHIPS | 126

Week 27: FEATURES OF ADOLESCENTS AGED BETWEEN SIXTEEN AND EIGHTEEN | 130

Week 28: MENTORING REFLECTIONS | 135

Week 29: MANAGING TIME EFFECTIVELY | 140

Week 30: MOTIVATE MENTEES | 144

Week 31: FAMILY AND SUPPORTIVE NETWORKS | 148

Week 32: FEEDBACK IS IMPORTANT | 153

Week 33: COACH STRENGTH-BASED STRATEGIES | 157

Week 34: MORE CHALLENGES | 162

Week 35: MENTORING REFLECTIONS | 167

Week 36: THE DIFFICULT CONVERSATIONS | 171

Week 37: CREATE MEANINGFUL RELATIONSHIPS | 175

Week 38: ALL ABOUT GOALS | 180

Week 39: DEVELOPMENTAL RELATIONSHIPS | 184

Week 40: BUILDING SELF-CONFIDENCE | 189

Week 41: A GROWTH MINDSET | 194

Week 42: MENTORING REFLECTIONS | 198

Week 43: DEVELOP RESILIENT YOUTH | 203

Week 44: EMPATHY AND TRUST | 208

Week 45: THE POWER OF CONNECTION | 212
Week 46: MENTORING QUALITIES REVISITED | 217
Week 47: CHAMPION GOAL ACHIEVERS | 221
Week 48: MENTORS AND SIGNIFICANT ADULTS | 225
Week 49: MENTORING REFLECTIONS | 230
Week 50: INVEST IN A LIFE | 234
Week 51: THE INSPIRED LEADER | 238
Week 52: FINAL REFLECTIONS | 242

Acknowledgments | 251
Bibliography | 253

FOREWORD

Robin Cox has spent more than two decades teaching and writing about youth mentoring in Australia, New Zealand, and Africa. Mentoring Minutes is a powerful culmination of his research, personal experiences and knowledge of the journey of mentors and mentees and what is required to build and ensure a sustainable mentoring relationship.

As a pioneer in the creation of school-based mentoring in America thirty-five years ago and an international consultant on mentoring, I have learned that dedicated, committed and caring mentors want to make a difference in the life of a young person but they cannot work in a vacuum. Much like their mentees, they must also feel supported, nurtured, inspired, and uplifted. Many programs are experiencing a high attrition rate among mentors. There may be many contributing factors but one my colleagues and I hear frequently is that the mentors are not sure if they are making a difference, sometimes feel isolated, and may not have adequate answers to their questions and concerns. They need to be reminded frequently that much of what they are experiencing with their mentee is normal, and be encouraged regularly not to give up.

Mentoring Minutes in some respects has become an almost self-help book for mentors. In this regard, it is a unique and revolutionary approach. In the book, Cox offers an incredibly valuable resource for mentors as they celebrate the growth and achievements of their mentees. The daily messages become a calendar of ongoing training, advice, encouragement, and hope. Each message instructs mentors on mentees' growth, development, feelings and needs and what they are experiencing as they go through the journey of life. Mentors are equipped with many tips and strategies to help mentees achieve their goals.

Cox offers a plethora of ways to create meaningful mentoring relationships between mentors and mentees. One of my favorite quotes comes from Carl W. Buehner in 1971. "They may forget what you said—but they will never forget how you made them feel." Mentoring Minutes is an instructional guide to making mentees feel self-worth, sense of belonging, get a better perspective on themselves, and the benefit of someone believing in them.

On any given day, a mentor can read a daily message and find comfort and encouragement. Every message is an invitation to mentors not to be afraid to try new ideas and strategies with their mentees. Given that a mentor is a friend and not a teacher, psychologist, counselor, or parent, the Dos and Don'ts are sure to create boundaries and lead to successful mentoring. It is also convenient that due to the book's intentional layout, the reader can enjoy a message or two at a time, select from the Table of Contents and be guided by the lessons. Mentors will be able to walk in their mentee's shoes and support them as their number one cheerleader.

Mentoring Minutes goes beyond the mentor/mentee audience. Most of the writings can be used as well by parents and teachers working with young people. The contents are practical and universal. The benefits to mentors and others remind me of a wonderful phrase in E.B. White's Charlotte's Web. "Why did you do all this for me?" Wilbur asked. Charlotte replied, "You have been my friend. By helping you, perhaps I was trying to lift up my life a trifle."

I applaud Robin Cox for writing Mentoring Minutes. Mentors and mentees and others as well will be inspired and uplifted by his messages of support, challenge, love, and affirmation.

Dr. Susan G. Weinberger
President, Mentor Consulting Group, USA

PREFACE
A Mentor's Dream

A few years ago, I was asked what I would say to a young person to encourage them to reach their potential. This is what I wrote:

My dream for you is that you wake up each morning, look at yourself in the mirror, love from the heart the person you see, always strive to be your unique self, and take a positive attitude into every day.

My dream for you is that you build your life on strong foundations, so that you can withstand the inevitable storms of life, and remain a positive person.

My dream for you is that you dare to dream big dreams, set realistic, achievable and measurable goals, fail sometimes, but remain determined to conquer adversity, and to discover, develop, and use your special gifts and talents to bring about a better community, a more caring society, a more compassionate world.

My dream for you is that you often take time out to reflect on your progress, to visualize yourself ten years from now as a happy, proud, yet humble person, content with life, continually placing the interests of others before your own.

My dream for you is that you discover the meaning of true love; that you sensibly risk entering into positive and meaningful relationships with others, and that your life is wonderfully enriched as a consequence.

My dream for you is that you remember that you are a beautiful person both on the inside and the outside; that you have potential greatness within you, and that, as you leave your footprints on the sands of life's journey, many will walk positively after you, and strive to emulate all that you achieve as a positive person of influence.

My dream for you is that you always remember that you are a special person in God's eyes, and that you discover, during your life's journey, His unique purpose for placing you on this planet.

My dream for you is everything that you positively wish for yourself![1]

1. Cox, *The Spirit of Mentoring*, 24.

THE SPIRIT OF MENTORING —A CALL TO ACTION

> Grace is a word with a stoop in it. Love reaches out on the same level, but grace reaches down to pick us up.
>
> —Author unknown

Why are you interested in youth mentoring?

This is an important question, as many well-intentioned people express an interest in mentoring youth, yet their motivation and understanding of youth is limited. Many volunteer adult mentors continue to move alongside young people and encourage them to chase their dreams, and reach their potential. The global community is enriched by the generosity of these people.

The best way to prepare yourself to mentor young people is to attend a mentor training program in which you travel on an experiential journey with other potential mentors to decide whether or not you are suited to youth mentoring. If not, there will be another way you can reach out and encourage people. Your unique gifts will never be wasted when you reach out to others.

Although youth mentoring has a long history, researchers and other professionals who work with youth continue to analyze how effective it is, and what form it should take.

Often, we have no idea how effective a mentoring relationship is. Then we read Matt's[1] story and how his mentor helped him transform his life, and we have a sense of the power of mentoring:

> Jim was the father figure and male role model I unconsciously needed at the time. He was always there for me, through the good times and the bad. He was never too busy to talk to me when I had a problem. He offered me advice on everything from academics

1. Barrett, *little moments*.

and athletics to girls. Jim had faith in me when I didn't have faith in myself. He believed in me so much growing up that I started to believe in myself.

WHY THIS BOOK?

When I moved to New Zealand in 1999, I became involved in the development of youth mentoring programs which focused on the building of developmental relationships as advocated a number of years later by Search Institute CEO Kent Pekel[2]:

> Search Institute's studies of developmental relationships are certainly confirming that caring is critical. However, while we found that caring is necessary, we are also learning that it is not sufficient to make a relationship truly developmental. In addition to expressing care, we have identified four other elements that are essential: challenging growth, providing support, sharing power and expanding possibilities. Taken together, those five elements are the pillars of our Developmental Relationships Framework.

Later I developed the school-based GR8 Mates youth mentoring programs in Australia, while continuing to contribute ideas and resources to other start-up youth *mentoring* programs in Australia, New Zealand, and Africa. The success of these programs was because they focused on some of the relational variables mentioned by psychologist Professor Jean Rhodes[3]—"counsel or empathy, genuineness and warmth; counselor direct influence skills on youth; youth willingness to participate." Jean shared a couple of points which my own experiences support:

> Mentors should be provided training in these universal characteristics of effective helping relationships, as relational bonds and the delivery of more targeted and specific approaches to mentoring. When this balance is achieved, the mentoring relationship may be poised to better address the needs of today's youth.

During these years I set up a website as a response to many queries I received about youth mentoring, and wrote a number of books to promote the spirit of mentoring, and youth-based peer mentoring, with the strong focus on building developmental relationships.

---

2. Pekel, *Moving Beyond Relationships*, 6.
3. Rhodes and Christensen, *Want to double your efforts?* 4–5.

I retired from my teaching career and developed 260 free short podcasts to encourage anyone mentoring young people—http://www.mentoringmatters.buzzsprout.com

MENTORING MINUTES

Mentoring Minutes is a collation of years of research, as well as my experiences working with, and coaching over 1000 adolescents (and teachers)—in a variety of face-to-face relationships—and training over 1000 volunteer adult mentors from a variety of professions. Mentoring Minutes is linked to the most recent adolescent brain research.

My research of youth mentoring programs in a number of countries revealed that a major challenge of many programs was *how* to offer regular and ongoing training and support to their mentors, with the purpose of building meaningful developmental relationships with their mentees. I searched bookstores and other online resources and did not find anything to meet that specific need—and it is a need, highlighted in feedback I have received from mentors.

So, I decided to write this book, condense, update, convert the content of the podcasts into a user-friendly weekly reference of messages to fill this gap, and be an encouragement to mentors, and anyone else working with youth. I have included "Mentoring moments" at the end of each week.

MENTORING MOMENTS

"Mentoring moments" provide practical examples of how ordinary people, like me, are impacted by the power of the spirit of mentoring. Brief vignettes of my personal experiences as a mentor and mentee are woven through these "Mentoring moments."

Unlike many young people, I was fortunate to have some significant adults move quickly alongside me at crucial times of my childhood, after I had major cancer surgery as a young boy, followed soon after by the sudden death of my mother. Later, as I gained in self-confidence, I approached adults I respected for encouragement and support. In reality they became my mentors, and helped shape, refine, coach, and guide me to chase my dreams and fulfill my potential.

All these mentors and coaches during my youth had been trained to work with youth. Most would have attended professional development workshops to keep them informed of youth-related research. In some ways, they give credence to Professor Jean Rhodes'[4] belief that: "Rather than deliver interventions, mentors in nonspecific programs should be trained to support their mentee's engagement in targeted, evidence-based interventions."

These vignettes describe how my mentors sowed and nurtured the spirit of mentoring as they positively influenced different seasons of my life, and then how I have passed that mentoring baton on to others as best as I can. All the stories are true. The names of my mentors are their real names, though I have changed the names of those I have mentored to protect their privacy. Their actual words are shared, as examples of how to sow the seeds of the spirit of mentoring in the lives of those with whom we interact. Mentoring keeps me humble, and always open to new teaching.

I also share feedback from adolescent mentees, adolescent peer mentors, and volunteer adult mentors in these pages to highlight the power of mentoring our youth, and to encourage anyone with an interest in mentoring to take on an unforgettable challenge.

HOW TO USE THIS BOOK

This user-friendly book has *not* been written as a book to read from cover to cover. Here are some suggestions for you to obtain the best value from the book.

- The daily messages cover fifty-two weeks of the year. There are five messages each week, including the "Mentoring moments." The messages vary in length. I would encourage you to set up a discipline that works for you and allocate a few minutes to the days you read and reflect on the messages. You will feel more confident that you can develop a meaningful relationship with your mentee. Keep the book on your office desk, by your bed, or in a place where you can refer to it for a couple of minutes each day.

- The messages are arranged into general themes, which continue to work within a holistic framework—the development of the whole person. This structure allows you to use it as a reference should you want to look up a particular topic. However, if you are dealing with challenging issues, it is worth seeking the opinions of professionals, or more experienced people.

---

4. Rhodes, *Four takeaways*, 3.

- Parents and teachers of adolescents can remind themselves each day of the challenges young people face. Some strategies and tips will be helpful. A message can provide encouragement and important reinforcement of methods they use to build relationships with youth.

- Grandparents are important role models in the lives of young people, though can feel out of touch with the world of youth. These messages fill most of those gaps, and also reinforce the important mentoring role they can undertake in the lives of young people, many of whom turn naturally to the older generation for encouragement, guidance, and a sympathetic ear.

- The book can be used by youth mentoring programs, and other youth organizations as part of their ongoing training. The content can be used for discussion topics when groups of mentees meet during the mentoring experience.

- Schools and education institutions can use the book as a user-friendly resource for staff—including non-teaching staff—who interact with youth each day.

- You can add your own notes on the relevant pages and create a valuable mentoring reference book.

Each week begins with a well-known quote to encourage you to take a moment to reflect on your life, as well as the life of your mentee. Each daily message focuses on an aspect of youth mentoring linked to a weekly theme. The core topics covered are: an outline of the history of mentoring and its relevance in the lives of twenty-first century youth; how to become a great mentor; understanding youth issues; self-image; goal setting; communication; resiliency; and how to positively resolve conflicts.

Many strategies for the development and maintenance of a meaningful relationship with your mentee are offered. Each Mentoring Minute finishes with a "Mentoring tip"—a sentence or two which simply reinforces a key aspect of a quality mentoring relationship, and aims to encourage you, and remind you of your value as a youth mentor.

Mentors can adapt the ideas and thinking behind the messages to their communities, with the understanding that not all strategies and suggestions are applicable to youth mentoring programs offered within different socio-economic areas and cultural groups.

REPETITION OF CONTENT

There is repetition throughout the Mentoring Minutes messages. This is deliberate. Repetition is important if a mentoring relationship is to become meaningful and worthy of the time invested in it by the mentor and the mentee.

Repetition is also necessary because *every* relationship is unique and moves at a different pace for a variety of reasons which are explained in the Mentoring Minutes messages. These messages and the "Mentoring moments" take account of this reality.

A TRIBUTE TO MY MENTOR

Who were the most important and positive adults during your adolescence other than your parents—not the case in every young person's upbringing? Can you think of *the* most significant adult? Someone who took on a mentoring role as advocated by mentoring expert Dr. Susan Weinberger[5]:

> Mentors need to show their mentees that they really care about them. This can be accomplished when a mentor is there for a mentee, serves as their number one advocate, is a good listener, provides consistency and commitment to the relationship and is a friend, confidant, and nurturer. What is the most important role of a mentor? Be a good listener. I always say in my trainings: 'We have two ears and one mouth so listen twice as much as you talk.'

Anthony Mallett was my high school principal. He was my cricket coach when I was fifteen years of age. I was a student leader in his leadership team when I was seventeen, and then school captain (head student) in my final year of school. Anthony became my mentor during this particular season of my life.

Later, I spent two years as a student tutor at my old school while I completed my teaching degree, so Anthony and I had many opportunities to chat when our paths crossed. I also taught for two years at the school under Anthony's leadership.

Anthony was a superb teacher, brilliant sportsman and coach, a leader of some repute, and an exceptional actor. I will never forget the small role I had in a staff play when I was on stage with him—a laugh a minute for the audience and Anthony, certainly not for me!

---

5. Weinberger, *Preparing my Mentor*, 7.

THE SPIRIT OF MENTORING—A CALL TO ACTION

Anthony coached me how to think and strategize as a cricket captain, never to give up, and always play to win within the spirit of the game. He did not like to lose, yet modeled how to be gracious in defeat.

Anthony coached me to be true to myself, to have the courage of my convictions, to listen carefully to all sides of an argument, to stand tall in the face of adversity, never to fear respectfully sharing my thoughts and opinions with others, and to be a servant leader. He also coached me the importance of being teachable, to laugh often, and never to take life too seriously.

My final handwritten school report from Anthony has motivated and inspired me more times than I can remember. He saw something in me that I still sometimes struggle to see in myself. His comments continue to remind me never to accept a second-best effort, as well as the power of the written word, and the lifelong impact positive words can have.

> Robin's outstanding contribution to the school deserves the highest praise: he is a young man of deep sensitivity coupled with a tenacity of purpose that will make him a really able person. He has led his school by sheer example and personality; he has learnt to view situations broadly and to have his advice discarded in favor of the wider perspective. I shall miss him as a friend, and the school will miss him as a leader of considerable stature. Good luck—but not goodbye!

I became a school principal of a school in Cape Town situated less than ten minutes from Anthony's retirement home. He had taught at the school for a brief time after retiring as a school principal.

I will never forget a cold wintry afternoon when I was working late. Anthony must have seen the light on in my office. He often used to walk around the school grounds. A short, sharp knock on the door, and Anthony popped his head in. For the next half-an-hour or more he sat on the edge of my desk, and we chatted about education and life—the mentor and the mentee who now sat in the principal's chair.

My intention was to ask Anthony to mentor me in the months ahead. He was trustworthy, had a sharp mind, enjoyed a challenging conversation, and had much experience and wisdom to share. Sadly, soon after that visit Anthony's cancer gained a firm foothold on his body, and he died a few months later.

I know how proud he was to see one of his former students eventually become a school principal—now I pass on the legacy, as I echo the powerful words of business executive Lenny Springs[6]:

> We are still being mentored. If you look at each of us [in this organization], someone in our lives recognized us, told us that we could achieve and be somebody. Success doesn't just happen. It's not the luck of the draw. We are all standing on other people's shoulders. And I can't forget that. I won't forget it. That's why I give back, because someone paved the way for me.

Have you thought about whose shoulders you are standing on? Perhaps you have, and that is why you picked up this book.

I hope you enjoy and gain inspiration and encouragement from the Mentoring Minutes messages, and will continue to remind yourself—through the highs and lows of your relationship with your mentee—that every adolescent is a unique person with specific strengths, gifts, and talents that need to be nurtured and supported.

Thank you to all the amazing mentors within our global community who become the light in the darkness of others and, through their example, model the *spirit of mentoring*.

---

6. Dortch Jr., *The Miracles*, 132.

MENTORING MINUTES

WEEK 1 TO WEEK 52

When a fractured leg is healed
it must walk again;
when a damaged zipper is mended
it must zip again;
when a sagging gate is fixed
it must swing again,
and when a broken heart is mended
it must give again.

—Author unknown

Week 1

INTRODUCING MENTORING

Every child deserves a champion—an adult who will never give up on them, who understands the power of connection and insists that they become the best they can possibly be.

—Rita F. Pierson

DAY 1: WHAT IS A MENTOR?

The word mentor has Greek origins and means a "wise guide." Traditionally a mentor was an older, more experienced person who was responsible for coaching and mentoring a younger person to fill a particular role. In the Middle Ages, the new generation learned art, craft and commerce in a master-apprentice relationship—for example, the young apprentice learnt the art of making shoes from a shoemaker.

Today young men and women apprentices continue to learn a trade, or specific job skills from those more experienced than themselves.

A mentor takes on a more challenging role than that of a master who guides an apprentice. A mentor becomes both a friend and a role model to a mentee at a time in the young person's life when the influence of peers is of the utmost importance. The brain is at a critical stage of development, and many young people are unsure of friends, or adult support.

Missionary and teacher Ron Lee Davis stated that the value of the mentoring process lies in watching a person of genuine wisdom and character surmount obstacles, solve problems, and overcome mistakes. The secret to profoundly influencing others as a mentor lies in honestly and transparently opening our lives to inspection warts and all.

Mentoring tip: Let your mentee discover a mentor who teaches them to stretch, handle discomfort, fulfill dreams, and move out of their comfort zone.

DAY 2: ADOLESCENTS FEEL SAFE AND SECURE

Before we can effectively mentor adolescents, we should consider and understand the world in which they live. My research, spanning about two decades, states that adolescents want to be cared for and loved unconditionally.

Here are some ideas about the meaning of taking care of a young person.

- Adolescents wish to feel safe and secure.
- The more these adolescents feel cared for, the more secure they become.
- Adolescents are surrounded by people who care for, appreciate and accept them unconditionally; people who are aware that their brains are developing; there will be mood swings and inconsistent behavior patterns.
- Adolescents value the positive influences of peers and adults they trust to encourage them to fulfill their potential.
- Adolescents are encouraged to appreciate that they have a greater chance to reach their potential when clear rules or boundaries (some of which are negotiated) are in place. They understand that, when they choose to step over these boundaries, there will be reasonable consequences.

Well-known psychologist and youth mentoring expert Professor Jean Rhodes[1] wrote: "Shepherd Zeldin and colleagues reviewed more than 200 research studies and concluded that, in order to successfully pass through adolescence, youth need 'access to safe places, challenging experiences, and caring people on a daily basis.'"

Mentoring tip: Mentoring is a commitment—you invest in the future when you move alongside a young person as their non-judgmental cheerleader.

---

1. Rhodes, *Stand by Me*.

DAY 3: ADOLESCENTS FEEL VALUED

When researchers state that adolescents would like to be valued, what does this mean?

- The more adolescents feel valued, the more positive self-worth they experience.
- Adolescents want to be encouraged, and to feel they have some power and control over things that happen to them
- Adolescents who are guided by a mentor on a self-empowering journey feel valued, respected, liked, and regarded as significant resources.
- Adolescents value fun time to interact with peers and other adults. This involves the development of important social skills, made more vital as the digital age impacts their understanding of communication, body language, tone of voice, and gestures.

Kurt Hahn the great educator and founder of Outward Bound said: "There are three ways of trying to win the hearts of the young. There is persuasion, there is compulsion, and there is attraction. You can't preach at them. That is a hook without worms. You can say, "You must volunteer," and that is of the devil, and you can tell them, "You are needed," and that appeal hardly ever fails."

Mentoring tip: When your mentees feel they are valued and worth your time and effort, you are most likely to connect.

DAY 4: ADOLESCENTS KNOW THEIR LIVES HAVE MEANING AND PURPOSE

What do researchers mean when they state that adolescents want to know that life has meaning and purpose?

- Adolescents can take ownership of the fact that their lives have significance.
- The more adolescents understand that there is a reason for their existence, the more significant they feel.
- Adolescents value encouragement to explore opportunities within and outside of school or the workplace, to learn and develop new skills and interests. This is especially important as their brains develop.

- Adolescents are encouraged to acquire a commitment to learning: academic success and the long-term value of learning enhance their self-worth as they discover their gifts and talents.
- Adolescents can appreciate and understand how to make tough decisions and choices, and how to cope with new situations.
- Adolescents require guidance to develop a positive view of the future.

Mentors strive to build their mentees up, encourage, correct, and stretch them.

Mentors never hesitate to make themselves vulnerable with their mentees, and do their best to live and model sound morals and values.

Mentoring tip: Positively influence your mentee, and serve as a role model, and wise advocate.

MENTORING MOMENTS

I was diagnosed with cancer aged nine. During the next two years I underwent two major operations and months of radiotherapy, receiving twice the adult dose. In his journal, my father described me as "dangerously ill."

Peter Le Mesurier was my junior school teacher and sport coach. He wrote to my father before my first major operation to wish me well.

Many months later I was desperate to follow my passion and return to the sport fields. Peter understood my situation, protected me from danger, nurtured, coached, and inspired me to become a better player within a collaborative team environment.

Peter was a man of few words. However, he was a significant adult role model in my young life. He remained interested in my school and professional career until his death at an old age. Peter sowed the seeds of the spirit of mentoring in the life of a young boy desperately trying to find his way. I am indebted to his unconditional care and encouragement displayed to me throughout my life.

Mentoring tip: Significant adults in the lives of youth help them cross the bridge of personal growth from child to young adult in a safe and secure environment.

Week 2

DIFFERENT MENTORING ROLES

> Do not train a child to learn by force or harshness; but direct them to it by what amuses their minds, so that you may be better able to discover with accuracy the peculiar bent of the genius in each.
>
> —Plato

DAY 1: MENTORING JOURNEY

Here are a few thoughts about what mentors can do in non-threatening ways to make sure that their mentee always feels safe and secure in their presence.

- Find out if your mentee has a pet. Share thoughts about which animals fascinate you. Take a walk around the local zoo if this is a practical option.
- If appropriate, go and pick strawberries (or another seasonal fruit) together. Encourage your mentee to bring a friend along.
- Show your mentee the website of your current, or former workplace (where applicable).
- Attend a local sports game or cultural event together.
- Make a genuine effort to understand your mentee's social structures if your mentoring relationship is cross-cultural.
- Broaden your mentee's knowledge and provide opportunities to explore new situations, places, and cultures.

Finally, a valuable tip, and one that is often overlooked by mentors, is to make brief notes when you arrive home after a meeting with your mentee. This is a way to prepare for your next meeting, and improves the early challenge of making a positive connection. Consider questions like these: What have you talked about? What concerns has your mentee expressed? What special achievements has your mentee shared with you? What progress can you see in your mentee's personal development journey? What strengths does your mentee display? How are your mentee's friends or parents influencing them? Which are the most important (or influential) relationships in your mentee's life?

Mentoring tip: Celebrate your mentors and share your mentoring experiences with your mentee at every opportunity—powerful coaching.

DAY 2: MENTORING RESEARCH

Significant youth mentoring research has been carried out over the past thirty to forty years. The jury is still out on the *effectiveness* of different youth mentoring programs—community programs, school-based programs, programs for youth from high-risk environments, or with significant mental health issues.

Most of the credible research has been undertaken in America and Canada where youth mentoring is decades ahead of other countries. However, what I discovered when I visited twenty-two youth mentoring programs in these two countries on a Churchill Fellowship a few years ago, was that many programs offered fairly average mentor training to prepare their volunteer mentors for the mentoring journey.

Training is significant for mentors of adolescents to understand the world of youth—the different environments in which they live, how vulnerable they are, what makes them tick, how the brain develops, as well as explore effective strategies which lead to positive outcomes at the conclusion of a mentoring journey.

Research highlights how important it is for young people to experience a variety of challenges, and to have access to safe places with a network of caring and supportive people around them.

Well-known youth mentoring expert and researcher Professor Jean Rhodes[1] has pointed out that once mentors and mentees have established an emotional bond—a key step in the mentoring journey—the mentors influence their mentees in three important ways.

1. Mentors enhance a mentee's social skills and emotional wellbeing.

---

1. Rhodes, *Stand by Me*, 35.

2. Mentors improve the cognitive skills of mentees through listening and effective communication.
3. Mentors serve as a role model, and an advocate for their mentee.

Mentoring tip: Never forget that you have something important to offer your mentee, which includes when and how to share life experiences.

DAY 3: THE VARIETY OF MENTORING ROLES

A grave mistake many mentors make is to believe that they can rescue or save their mentees. This thinking negatively impacts the mentoring relationship from the first day of meeting.

A mentor is not a cool peer, a parole officer, a foster parent, a bank or ATM machine, a mentee's scheming sidekick or private secretary, a taxi, parent, babysitter, disciplinarian, therapist, social worker, counsellor, or nag.

The positive, yet challenging and deeply satisfying mentor's role, involves wearing a variety of hats at different times: a friend, a motivator, a guide, a coach, a tutor, a companion, a resource, a confidant, a listener, a non-judgmental cheerleader, a role model, a supporter, an advocate, a sounding board, a networker, or a negotiator. The role depends on what occurs in the mentee's life at a particular time.

Former American Secretary of Education Richard Riley[2] stated: "A mentor may be the person who makes the difference—by providing a role model for positive behaviors, like studying hard and staying away from trouble, by helping with academic work, by encouraging the student to take the right college-preparatory courses, or by providing extra moral support and encouragement—in short, by saying, 'Yes, you can do it—you can achieve your dreams . . .'"

Mentoring tip: You have connected when your mentee becomes a valued friend.

DAY 4: WHAT A MENTOR DOES

Every mentoring relationship is different. Here are some examples of what might be involved in a youth mentoring relationship.

- Become a wise, trusted, and dependable friend.

2. United States Education Department, *Yes You Can*.

- Have fun as you do something worthwhile.
- Focus on the needs of your mentees.
- Encourage a caring, supportive, non-judgmental relationship. The mentor is the consistent cheerleader, or the wise guide on the side.
- Encourage mentees to reach their potential.
- Recognize the difference between accepting mentees and approving of their behavior. For example, love and care for mentees, and disapprove of inappropriate behavior.
- Empower your mentees with key life skills.
- Express your thoughts and feelings positively and assertively.
- Learn to respond with kindness, compassion, and forgiveness where appropriate.
- Choose an appropriate time to talk about an issue and select your words carefully.
- Help to create a clear action plan with realistic, specific, and achievable goals that mentees own.
- Spend time with mentees and interact regularly in order to enhance their self-worth, pride, and confidence.
- Encourage mentees to be proactive and coach them how to carefully weigh up consequences before they take action.

Mentoring tip: Consistently accountable mentors build trust with their mentees and are positive role models.

MENTORING MOMENTS

When my wife and I became engaged, I received a note from Ken, a student I had coached sport, and mentored for a couple of years. It highlights the importance for mentors to enjoy the interactions with youth, and never to take oneself too seriously. Ken wrote:

> Sincere congratulations. Fantastic news. Wow! This is just a short note to say well played, it must have been all the fitness training! . . . best wishes to the lucky lady.
>
> When the moment comes
> and you know it's yours

take it
and run with it
and turn it into a lifetime.
Turn that moment
into a lifetime—
nobody can stop you.
(William Hagar)

Ken concluded his note and informed me of his selection for a state sports team—a goal achieved.

Mentoring tip: Always remind youth that you are present in their lives to encourage them to fulfill their heart's desires.

Week 3

MENTORS AS ROLE MODELS

The best teachers are those who tell you where to look, but don't tell you what to see.

—Alexandra K. Trenfor

DAY 1: MEET YOUR MENTEE

The early stages of a mentoring relationship are the most challenging. Two strangers, unique, gifted, and talented individuals of different ages, and from different backgrounds come together to embark on a journey into the unknown.

Set out to create a nurturing and supportive relationship. Your mentee must feel affirmed and encouraged at all times.

During the early stages of the mentoring journey you—as the adult—set the tone of the meetings. Establish yourself as a positive role model, and place some clear boundaries in the relationship with which you and your mentee are comfortable—negotiate these. You share your values as you share your life story. Make sure you back these up with consistent behavior and actions.

Assist your mentee to share thoughts about what is right and wrong. Do not be afraid to chat to your mentee if you feel their behavior is inappropriate. Point out why you feel the way you do, and share thoughts about more appropriate behavior.

Listen to your mentee and encourage them to think about the future. You assist them to set personal, achievable, and realistic goals, a fun and often rewarding experience for both parties.

Mentoring tip: Mentoring relationships are often one-sided initially. You, not your mentee, are responsible for keeping the relationship alive.

DAY 2: MENTORS ARE ROLE MODELS

Every mentoring relationship is different. Here are a few pointers about how you can strive to become an exemplary mentor to youth—there are no perfect mentors.

- Encourage, coach, and inspire mentees to develop their personal visions for the future.
- Express your personal feelings verbally and through body language, such as an authentic smile, laughing out loud, communicating disappointment, anger, or sadness in your voice and facial expressions.
- Feel secure and unthreatened in the face of a mentee's ambivalent attitudes or strong feelings.
- Wherever possible work with the mentee's family, or caregivers, or teachers, or employer, to provide them with support, friendship, encouragement, reinforcement, constructive and honest feedback, and wise counsel.
- Encourage mentees to recognize the importance of a sound education, and to see the links between studies, career training and future career, professional fields of interests or hobbies.
- Assist mentees to enter the workplace and understand employer expectations about attitude, preparedness, appearance, teamwork, and skills required for the particular job.

Mentoring tip: Provide a safe space for your mentee to share sensitive issues. Young people appreciate sincere guidance and encouragement from a non-parent adult they respect and can trust.

DAY 3: KEY AREAS OF A MENTOR'S ROLE

> Adolescence is a period for loosening home ties, exploring the world outside the family, trying out new roles, and learning to be independent. Traversing this difficult terrain successfully is facilitated by the presence of trusted adults to whom youth can turn for guidance and support. Through interactions with others, particularly supportive adults, youth acquire the skills necessary for successfully negotiating the world at large.
>
> —Cynthia Sipe[1]

1. Delpit, *The Politics*.

With these words in mind, consider four key areas a trusted, supportive mentor can explore with their mentee during the mentoring journey.

1. Mentors offer academic help. They provide *practical* help. Link the mentee with someone who can assist them, while you explore and identify resources with your mentee.
2. Mentors involve themselves in a career exploration journey. Find out what the mentee is curious about; arrange job shadowing; encourage internet research; conduct informational interviews with your mentee, and explore opportunities and interests together.
3. Mentors provide social experiences. Take your mentee out of the neighborhood, and expose them to as many cultural and recreational experiences as possible.
4. Mentors offer emotional support. Pay attention and show genuine concern towards your mentee which the latter might lack in their personal environment; be the trusted adult your mentee can talk to about issues they are uncomfortable discussing with their parents or caregivers.

Mentoring tip: Great mentors explore their mentees' worlds together, dream their dreams, and inspire them to turn these dreams into reality.

DAY 4: CONNECT WITH YOUR MENTEE

A mentor must allow the relationship with their mentee to evolve. Be realistic about the time required. Do not expect miracles—teenagers are experiencing one of the most confusing periods of their lives.

Start with the non-threatening getting-to-know you process, which is likely to reveal some of your mentee's interests. Armed with this knowledge, conversations can progress to a straightforward goal setting journey. Your mentee must "always" take ownership of their goals.

Your mentee might test you during the early months, especially if they have been let down by a number of adults over a period of time. Be clear about your mentoring role. Negotiate clear boundaries. Never quit on your mentee.

After about six months (sooner for some mentors, later for others) your relationship moves to a deeper and more trusting level. Your mentee appreciates your genuine affirmations and looks forward to your interactions.

Never compare your mentoring relationship to others. Remember that you are the adult in the relationship. You might have to drive things during the early stages of the mentoring journey. Make sure that your mentee always feels safe and secure when they meet with you.

Mentoring tip: Mentoring involves opening your heart, and inviting your mentee to share your life. It is fun!

MENTORING MOMENTS

Fifteen-year-old Mason reflected on a nine-month mentoring relationship with his mentor, Ruth, in a school-based mentoring program:

> From this mentoring journey I learnt a lot of things such as, what I wanted to do for my future career and how I was going to achieve the goals I set for myself. The mentoring journey has also showed me how I could improve my life so I wasted a lot less time on things that didn't matter, and I decided to use that time to help myself achieve my long-term goals. I don't think I could have achieved this without the help of my mentor and this mentoring program.

Ruth wrote:

> I have enjoyed sharing this journey with Mason. I have seen him grow in confidence and self-belief. He has made positive changes in his daily life, has discovered a career path that interests him, and has become more assertive. I have enjoyed his sense of humor. I wish him well for his future and know that if he continues to believe in himself, he will accomplish more than he ever dreamed of.

Mentoring tip: Share the virtue of kindness with youth with whom you interact, and encourage them to pass it on to others.

Week 4

YOUTH CULTURE

The heart of mentoring—getting the most out of life isn't about how much you keep for yourself, but how much you pass on to others.

—David Stoddard[1]

DAY 1: UNDERSTAND YOUTH CULTURE (1)

The context of your mentee's life is important to understand so you appreciate what they cope with each day. Spend some time and reflect on what it was like to be the age of your mentee. Think about these questions:

- What was a typical day like?
- What was really important to you at that time?
- What were your parents, or caregivers like? Did you get along? Were you close?
- Think of your friends. Were friendships always easy, or were they sometimes hard? Why was this?
- In general, did you feel that adults understood you well?

At the same time, remember that some things change dramatically. The new generation may live in a context and have experiences that are vastly different from those of the previous generation. Today, for example, there may be significantly more alcohol and drug abuse compared to your youth; more widespread and dangerous sexually transmitted diseases; more crime and violence, particularly in urban areas; violence in the media, and in "games" as a commonplace event; the impact of the digital age—all the

---

1. Stoddard, *The Heart*.

positives and negative issues or factors; more single-parent families, and greater demands on all families.

Mentoring tip: Empathetically confront your mentee, and always remember your childhood experiences.

DAY 2: UNDERSTAND YOUTH CULTURE (2)

It is important to know the individual members of your mentee's family wherever possible. Visit the family at their home. Become involved in social activities within the community, and you gain the opportunity to share ideas, views, and values. You also develop a deeper understanding of their culture. Much will depend, of course, on the nature of your mentoring program—is it a community or school-based program, for example?

The socioeconomic background of your mentee could also differ markedly from your own, as stated in these examples.

- You own a house, while your mentee's family rents one.
- You own a car, while your mentee travels on public transport.
- You have a TV and DVD player, while your mentee has neither.
- You own a computer, while your mentee has no computer, has to share a room with two siblings, and lacks the privacy to work on their own.
- You have lived in the same house for five years, while in the same time your mentee has moved four times.

In other words, remember that many things you take for granted are not necessarily owned or experienced by others.

Poverty may cause stress and depression for your mentee. It may also create a different attitude to money. For example, your mentee might spend $100 on label clothes in order to enjoy the moment, as they do not believe there is any chance of a better future. There is no motivation to save money. However, you can sensitively help your mentee to create a new future for themselves, as you care for them in a non-judgmental, unconditional way.

Mentoring tip: Always respect the rules of your mentee's home, or school, or workplace.

DAY 3: TOMORROW'S YOUTH

A mentor shared a reason they chose to mentor: "Looking after the children and youth of today will influence the quality of life for me tomorrow."

This is an interesting comment, a reminder of how valuable it is to invest our time and energy in the lives of youth in the hope that they will make a positive difference in the world.

Many adolescents complain that no-one listens to them. Consider these words written by American writer and management consultant Margaret Wheatley: "Listening is such a simple act. It requires us to be present and that takes practice, but we don't have to do anything else. We don't have to advise, or coach, or sound wise. We just have to be willing to sit there and listen."

We invest our time in youth, and we must work hard to become great and respected listeners.

Mentoring expert Bobb Biehl[2] provides another perspective: "Mentoring is a movement for quiet people who enjoy working behind the scenes for no pay or glory, just helping other people win."

My mentoring experiences have taught me that we are all winners. The relationship spins off into the school or work environment, time spent with peers, and often results in positive developments within family relationships.

Mentoring tip: Mentors display patience, that quality of endurance that can reach breaking point and not break.

DAY 4: PRODUCTIVE MENTORS

Mentoring expert and psychologist Marsha Sinetar[3] wrote a fascinating book in which she highlighted some key signs of productive mentors. These signs are relevant for all mentors of young people.

- Mentors affirm life and further its potential.
- Mentors enter into authentic dialogue because, at heart, they are genuinely and emotionally available.
- Mentors set clear boundaries for themselves and those they mentor.

---

2. Biehl, *Mentoring*.
3. Sinetar, *The Mentor's Spirit*, 146.

- Mentors "walk the talk," as they embody values and virtues others merely talk about, yet do not model.
- Mentors stabilize their mentees in a continuity of effort because they themselves are stable and grounded.

Educator and author Sheryl Feinstein[4], who has done extensive work with regard to the adolescent brain, highlighted the needs of youth, and the significance of a meaningful mentoring relationship: "Adolescence is a pivotal time in a person's development. The changes teens experience determines much about who they are—their work ethic, self-esteem, morality—and who they will become. This, in turn, shapes our society."

Mentoring tip: Set out to become an exemplary role model. Walk the talk. Live the values you coach. Your mentee will respect you, perhaps even strive to emulate you.

MENTORING MOMENTS

The adolescent years are a time of confusion at some point for most of our youth as they seek meaning and purpose in their lives, and explore the meaning of independence.

For a brief season I shared thoughts and ideas with fourteen-year-old Meg, now a successful business woman married with children. Meg shared these thoughts when I moved from the school. They continue to keep me humble, yet motivated to speak to the potential greatness of youth.

> This is just a small thank you note to express how much I appreciate everything you have done for this school and ultimately myself. I have never come across a principal as dynamic before, and I certainly hope [your successor] will be just as patient and dynamic as you were. I wish you the best of luck with your new job, although I'm sure you won't even need it. I am sure you'll fascinate the students at your future school as you have fascinated me.

Mentoring tip: You share your strengths and values as you share your life stories with youth.

---

4. Feinstein, *Secrets*, 165.

Week 5

CONNECT WITH YOUTH

A mentor empowers a person to see a possible future and believe it can be obtained.

—Shawn Hitchcock

DAY 1: POSITIVE SOCIAL INTERACTION

I enjoyed working alongside mentors and watching them embark on a mentoring journey with their adolescent mentees. I have never had to change mentors after the matching process has been completed, though this highlights the importance of such a process, and the importance of effective mentor training prior to the match.

How did we match mentors with young people?

Mentors and potential mentees participated in some non-threatening, fun activities. Then we ran something similar to a speed-dating activity. During this activity each mentee had a short time to chat with each mentor. Then the mentees confidentially wrote down their top three mentor choices, and the mentors did likewise with regard to the mentees. I was always able to give both the mentor and mentee their number one or two choice. This resulted in connections taking place relatively quickly, usually during the five-week probationary period, as I called the early stage of the mentoring journey.

It is a privilege to witness the inspiration, genuine pride, and joy expressed by the mentors as they became more involved in the mentoring journey. Some mentors openly expressed how their own self-esteem had been enhanced as a result of the mentoring experience. They had been given fresh insights into their own adolescent journeys. Other mentors described how their mentoring relationships had transformed their attitudes in a positive way in the workplace.

Mentoring tip: Continue to develop your mentee's cognitive skills through open, honest communication, and effective listening (lots of it!).

DAY 2: WAYS TO CONNECT WITH MENTEES (1)

The development of a meaningful and positive relationship with your mentee is a work in progress through the early stages of the mentoring journey. Much will depend on whether you are involved in a program within a community, or a school-based program. The latter will have some limitations. Some of these ideas will not be relevant in such situations.

- Encourage your mentee to write a journal in which they express personal thoughts, which they may or may not wish to share with you. Girls, more than boys, enjoy an activity like this.
- Encourage your mentee to join a local youth club, or faith group, or sport club, or cultural group.
- Find out who your mentee's friends are. You could do something as a group, which promotes a positive peer support group.
- Encourage inspirational reading (join the local library). Sometimes short articles, rather than books, will be of interest to a young person who does not enjoy reading.
- Share a recipe. Teach your mentee to bake or cook something. Exchange a cultural dish (where applicable).
- Do not impose your values on your mentee, but 'do' respect their family values (unless, of course, the family is involved in substance abuse, or some other antisocial behavior).
- Make a scrapbook of inspirational articles from newspapers, and magazines. Present it to your mentee at the end of the formal mentoring journey, or at another appropriate time.
- Spend time together and research careers your mentee is interested in, qualifications needed, subjects needed, and job opportunities available once qualifications are received. This activity often helps to encourage new goal setting ideas and gives meaning and purpose to a young life.
- Share photographs of your family, or pets, or travels with your mentee and their family. Share other photographs which might be relevant to discussions with your mentee.

- Talk about your respective choices of music—listen to each other's favorite songs or styles of music.

Remember at all times that mentoring must be fun. Laugh lots and take note of clinical professor of psychiatry and author Daniel J. Siegel's[1] wise words: "When we have supportive relationships, we are not only happier, we are healthier and live longer."

Mentoring tip: Create new opportunities and learning experiences for your mentee when you spend time together. You enrich a young life.

DAY 3: WAYS TO CONNECT WITH MENTEES (2)

Well-known Australian psychologist Andrew Fuller[2] wrote: "Feeling that you belong at your school was thought to be one of the major factors promoting wellbeing, self-esteem, and resilience in young people."

A key role of a mentor, where this is relevant, is to make sure that your mentee feels connected to the school community and with positive people within and outside of that community.

A connection with your mentee remains a work in progress. Do not be afraid to try new ideas or strategies. You soon discover whether or not these strategies contribute positively to the development of a positive mentoring relationship. Here are a few thoughts and ideas.

- Frame an accessible motivational saying that has inspired you and give it to your mentee. Share at least one of your life experiences in which this saying sustained you.
- Avoid embarrassing your mentee in front of their peers. Many mentees in some cultural groups prefer not to be praised publicly.
- Never criticize or rebuke your mentee in public.
- Affirm the uniqueness of your relationship with your mentee.
- Spontaneously send your mentee a message to indicate that you are thinking about them.
- Some research states that teenagers are less likely to share similar interests with their mentors. This will differ from relationship to relationship from what I have observed over the years. Some mentees

---

1. Siegel, *Brainstorm*, 8.
2. Fuller, *Raising Real People*.

select their mentor because the mentor *does* have a shared interest. Be patient and tolerant.

- Do not give medication to your mentee.
- Respect your mentee's faith or spiritual doctrines, and values.

Mentoring tip: Great mentors commit to see through the mentoring journey and are determined to make a positive contribution to their mentees' lives.

DAY 4: THE YOUNG PERSON'S BRAIN

Mentors continually remember that the adolescent brain undergoes a significant time of development that is only completed in their mid-twenties. The brain acts like a sponge as it soaks up new information and constantly changes to make room for it, a concept referred to as plasticity.

Plasticity assists youth to pick up new skills. For example, the potential novelist starts to write with vigor; the future basketball or netball stars start to achieve great things because of their positive attitude to the team or to practicing; the musician starts to develop new musical abilities, and the tech wizard starts to create new games.

A youth's brain needs more time and experience to develop, so continually affirm the "efforts" of your mentees.

Ronald E. Dahl from the University of Pittsburgh Medical Centre describes the teenage years of brain development: ". . . like turbocharging an engine without a skilled driver." Think of a mentor who takes on the role of the skilled driver and makes sure their mentees are safe. This allows vulnerable youth to move out of their comfort zones and to fail while daring greatly. Mentors provide the safety net.

Mentoring tip: Coach your mentees to be teachable, and never to quit when the going becomes tough.

MENTORING MOMENTS

Sheilah Wolfe was my grade one teacher a couple of years before she retired. She put clear boundaries in place, which seven-year-old boys needed, yet we felt safe and secure in her company at all times.

Sheilah had a magnificent Alsation dog, Allanah, which accompanied her to class on a few occasions. Sheilah never married, adored her dog, and was an inspiring teacher who never accepted a second-rate effort.

When I underwent my operations to remove cancer, Sheilah followed my progress. She gave me a wonderfully illustrated book on wild animals which I treasured for over fifty years.

At the end of my school career, ten years after Sheilah had taught me, she sent a card wishing me well: "Congratulations on your successes this year. I felt most proud of you . . . From Sheilah Wolfe with love and very happy memories."

Sheilah guided me through my first year of junior school. She believed in me, and encouraged me to chase my dreams and reach my potential. She was the wise guide on the side throughout my school career, a mentor, and a cherished friend.

Mentoring tip: Consistently strive to encourage your mentee to exercise excellence at all times—this builds resilience.

Week 6

FEATURES OF ADOLESCENTS AGED BETWEEN ELEVEN AND NINETEEN

> A mentor is someone who sees more talent and ability within you, than you see in yourself, and helps bring it out of you.
>
> —Bob Proctor

DAY 1: FEATURES OF ADOLESCENTS AGED BETWEEN ELEVEN AND NINETEEN (1)

At the beginning of the mentoring journey we remember our teenage experiences, for those experiences help us determine the shape of our mentoring journey with youth.

Here are some key features of adolescents between the ages of eleven and nineteen years.

- It is a precocious, unstable time.
- It is a time of rapid physical growth and human development changes:
  - Physical changes, triggered by rapid alterations in hormone production, are accompanied by growth changes.
  - The level of physical strength in boys effectively doubles between the ages of twelve and seventeen years.
  - Height increases dramatically in both boys and girls. Often the initial result is a slender look but, when growth slows, body weight tends to increase, which can lead to eating disorders.
  - Emotional maturity tends to lag behind physical development, which is why some adolescents seem very childish at times.

- It is a time of excitement, often associated with the pleasure of developing new abilities and talents. Physical changes can lead to storm and stress, an identity crisis, expanded cognition and moral reasoning, and belief in their own indestructibility. It can also cause inexplicable mood swings—one or more mood swing cycles per day, for example, anger, apathy, boredom, sadness, guilt, fear and anxiety, stress, joy and elation, love, experimentation with new behaviors, egocentric self-focus, idealism, movement away from parents, or movement towards peers.
- It is a time when the brain continues to develop, a process that is only completed when the young person is in their mid-twenties.

Mentoring tip: Expect your mentee to change in positive ways, and the change occurs as the right strategies are found.

DAY 2: FEATURES OF ADOLESCENTS AGED BETWEEN ELEVEN AND NINETEEN (2)

Here are more key features of adolescents between the ages of eleven and nineteen years to help us better understand the youth we mentor.

- Adolescents have a developing interest—often secretive—in the opposite sex and in sexuality in general. Their interest in same-sex peer groups decreases, while their focus on building friendships and dating relationships with members of the opposite sex increases.
- Some major social shifts take place as friends and peers become more important than family or extended family. Parental influences are temporarily abandoned as youth seek affiliations with their peer groups. (The first five years of life are crucial, particularly in regard to our relationships with the significant adults in our lives. All conclusions about our world and how we see ourselves in relationship to it are built on our earlier experiences and the decisions we made then. Did I receive positive or negative messages? Who am I? What is my world like? Have I experienced an interrupted love process? Do I fear abandonment?) Adolescents move from a state of dependence on the home to a state of interdependence. They keep the home contact as they develop other peer relationships. Attention-getting behavior creates feelings of significance and importance. Their quest for a personal

identity might propel them towards identification with hero images, which can have both positive and negative repercussions.

- If youth conform to the demands of peers, they are less likely to be the target of unwelcome attention. Never underestimate the audience factor, as youth ask themselves: What do others think of me?

Mentoring tip: Effective mentors help their mentees to appreciate that every young person is responsible for the choices they make during their life journey.

DAY 3: FEATURES OF ADOLESCENTS AGED BETWEEN ELEVEN AND NINETEEN (3)

Here are more important features of youth aged between eleven and nineteen years.

- Peers are seen as more legitimate sources of authority than parents on matters of dress, hairstyle, smoking or vaping, alcohol, sex, drug-taking, driving, money, fringe petty crime, music, films, use of technology, and decisions concerning how late to stay out, or what to do at the weekend.

- In later adolescence, individuals formulate their own value system. Strands of parental values are combined with values gained personally through boundary testing and experimentation across a variety of areas. They become more comfortable with their "new" body, and focus their energies on future issues such as vocational education or relationship commitments.

- Early teenage years are a mixture of a desire for freedom and wanting structure and protection. Youth often find adult activities and interests boring, as they develop into independent young adults.

- 88 per cent of youth say they like their parents and expect them to nag at times, as nagging shows an expression of love and care.

- Two parents whose value systems differ sow more confusion in an adolescent's life.

Mentoring tip: If you want to watch your mentee grow several meters before your eyes, offer authentic, and positive feedback.

DAY 4: FEATURES OF ADOLESCENTS AGED BETWEEN ELEVEN AND NINETEEN (4)

Adolescents aged between the ages of eleven and nineteen tend to respond in the following ways to the variety of issues in their lives.

- Schools with benevolent dictatorships are effective!
- Young people want adults to
  - listen—provide individual attention to youth, and take them seriously;
  - be available;
  - be non-judgmental, and have non-directive attitudes; consult more;
  - retain a sense of humor;
  - be a straight talker so that youth know where they stand;
  - be trustworthy, and observe confidentiality.
- The higher the parents' socioeconomic status, the higher the average levels of literacy and home language performance of their children (boys and girls).
- The family or extended family environment has a stronger influence on education achievement than socioeconomic status. Reflect on these points.
  - Where a family income declines, the child's overall academic competence also declines.
  - Divorce can lead to a fall in socio-economic status, which, in turn, might affect a child's outcomes.
  - Australian research stated that the proportion of children in sole parent families with low academic competence is almost twice as high as the proportion of those in couple families.
  - Children in stepfamilies tend to perform less well academically.
  - Divorce (as shown in Australian research) has more enduring negative consequences for boys than for girls possibly due to the absence of a male role model. This suggests a lack of consistent discipline.

- Sole parent families, despite the inherent difficulties they face, may also raise their children well and successfully, though on average the risks are greater.

Mentoring tip: Great mentors "always" celebrate their mentees' growth and achievements.

MENTORING MOMENTS

Fourteen-year-old Jacob was struggling to find his way. His parents had divorced and both had married new partners. Jacob was lost and lonely in a boarding house.

Twenty years later he contacted me to thank me for moving alongside him. This is Jacob's story:

> Thought I would drop you a line and hear how you are. I often think of you and how you voluntarily took me under your wing, so to speak during my time at [the school], encouraging and guiding me through the often irrational and rudderless years of one's teens! One incident sprang to mind. During my grade seven year, when I was opening and locking the club room, for which you awarded me a generous portion of service points (many thanks!!), you recommended I read Eric Liddle's biography [the story on which the film, *Chariots of Fire* was based]. In retrospect the story had a profound effect on my psyche... I am extremely grateful for all you did for me: all those hours when you threw to me in the cricket nets, and I would sometimes manage to straight bat a ball out of the front, and off you would jog to fetch it. I would like you to know that your actions have had a positive, material effect on my life, both in a faith and sporting sense. Although I only played a handful of games for the university first cricket team, I think I achieved my potential on the [other sport] field, and you were a big motivation behind that.

Jacob's story reminds mentors that the true impact of many mentoring relationships might only be known many years later, and after the mentee pauses to reflect on their life journey. This is a critical point many sponsors of youth mentoring programs fail to understand, as they expect a "quick-fix" solution to the challenges which youth face.

Mentoring tip: You are a courageous pioneer as you venture into the unexplored territory of a youth's life. What an exciting challenge!

Week 7

MENTORING REFLECTIONS

My mentor said, "Let's do it," not, "You do it."

—Jim Rohn

DAY 1: MENTORING ADOLESCENTS FROM HIGH-RISK ENVIRONMENTS

There might be occasions when you wonder, as a mentor of an adolescent mentee living within a high-risk environment, whether you genuinely can contribute much that is positive to this young life.

Let me share some ideas from youth mentoring research to encourage you either to keep on keeping on as a mentor, or to join a youth mentoring program focused on youth who live in high-risk environments, and where you receive professional support and encouragement.

- Encourage your mentees to reach their potential, and consistently speak positive messages of "hope" into their lives.
- Help and guide your mentees to become self-sufficient, productive citizens.
- Improve your mentee's conflict resolution skills.
- Guide your mentees towards more reliable and responsible attendance at school or work.
- Improve your mentee's social and communication skills in relationships with family, peers, and extended family. Also focus on behavior, attitudes, and appearance.
- Enhance a sense of social responsibility in your mentee's life.
- Encourage your mentees to make positive life choices.

- Develop positive values in your mentee's lives, often modeled most effectively by your exemplary attitude and lifestyle.
- Improve your mentee's self-image through your interactions with them.
- Expose your mentees to positive and new experiences, such as community involvement, and how to respectfully understand different cultures and activities.

Retired school principal and vertical tutoring systems expert Peter Barnard[1] reminds us how important networks are in a young person's life:

> From a child's point of view, it makes sense to be surrounded by a number of supportive personnel options and to have leadership, mentoring, and support on tap everywhere. The greater the number and availability of connections (nonlinear), the more stable, resilient, and adaptive the person and organization. Being better connected and supported all the time is a better means of building resilience than attending a pro-social program some of the time.

Mentoring tip: Sow a mentoring seed and reap a positive person of influence who could one day confidently impact the world.

DAY 2: MENTORS MOTIVATE AND INSPIRE

Well-known mentoring expert Rey Carr[2] points out that youth need additional adults in their lives to provide them with opportunities for the development of self-esteem, academic ability, and to learn how to become personally responsible for the choices they make: "Mentors can act as motivators, guides, and sources of inspiration to assist young people to successfully manage life experiences. Ultimately mentors can increase the likelihood that young people will benefit from educational services, reduce the possibility of leaving school early, and contribute to a successful transition between the school and work worlds."

Rey also shared: "A natural mentor is typically a person from outside of our family who plays an empowering role to help mentees achieve life goals and dreams, explore alternatives, and deal with life challenges."

---

1. Barnard, *Socially Collaborative Schools*, 81.
2. Carr, *Mentorship*.

Mentoring expert Dr. Susan Weinberger[3] highlights the power of mentoring:

> In the United States, chronic student absenteeism is a hidden educational crisis. It is associated with a variety of adverse consequences, including individual course failure, risk of not graduating, and poor socio-emotional outcomes. One promising strategy is to deliberately match mentors with students struggling with attendance. Once mentors know the source of the problem, they are helping students to find solutions through a variety of successful strategies. This is really good news.

Mentoring tip: Share your burning passions or ideas that drive your life with your mentee with empathy and sensitivity. "Always" be a positive person of influence.

DAY 3: PRESCRIPTIVE V DEVELOPMENTAL MENTORING

A mistake some mentors make is to enter a mentoring relationship with a prescriptive approach. When mentors follow a *prescriptive* approach, they might do one or more of the following:

- try to save or rescue the mentee;
- try to reform or transform the mentee by setting goals too early in the relationship;
- adopt more of a parental or authoritative role;
- emphasize behavior change more than develop the relationship with the mentee;
- have difficulty meeting with the mentee regularly and consistently;
- try to instill a set of values that are different from, or inconsistent with, those the mentee expects at home;
- ignore the advice of program staff, where a mentor is linked to a youth mentoring program.

Researchers state that after nine months only 30 percent of mentors and mentees in a prescriptive relationship meet regularly.

However, in a *developmental* relationship, these same researchers state that after nine months 91 percent of mentors and mentees continue to meet regularly.

3. Weinberger and Forbush, *The Role of Mentoring*, 80.

Here are some key aspects of a developmental relationship.

- The mentor involves the mentee in deciding how they spend their time together.
- The mentor and mentee make a commitment to be consistent and dependable.
- The mentor understands that the relationship might be fairly one-sided initially, but takes responsibility, as an adult, to keep the relationship alive.
- The mentor is determined to have fun.
- The mentor respects the mentee's opinions and viewpoints.

Mentoring tip: Play a supportive, encouraging, and strengthening role with your mentee.

DAY 4: SET PERFORMANCE GOALS

There are a range of processes for setting and achieving goals. Mentors encourage their mentees to experiment with different processes until they find one that works for them.

I tend to focus on performance goals when I work with youth, as I find mentees take ownership of their goals and, in most cases, go from strength to strength as they strive to reach their potential. Performance goals allow mentees to set processes in motion to achieve their eventual goal or outcome. Mentees control the process, though they cannot control the outcome.

- Performance goals follow a step-by-step process. This makes progress easier to measure.
- Performance goals are "behavior-oriented" and "specific."
- Performance goals allow flexibility when mentees hit major obstacles or setbacks.
- Performance goals lead to ongoing achievement, which increases the mentees' sense of self-worth, and confidence in their ability to repeat or improve on past efforts.
- Performance goals are challenging, yet realistic, and a valuable aspect of positive brain development.

Mentoring tip: Turn every mentoring experience into a learning opportunity.

MENTORING MOMENTS

Fifteen-year-old Matt struggled in my history class. This led to a discussion on how he could improve. We met for extra tuition each week over a nine-month period, at the end of which Matt had progressed from barely a pass to achieving a distinction in his final public exam.

During this time I also coached Matt on the sport field, so we had positive interactions away from an academic environment.

Matt's mother wrote me this note which highlighted the importance of a mentor as a patient, non-judgmental cheerleader, and encourager.

> We cannot thank you enough for all the help, interest, and time you have so willingly given Matt this year. He was, as you know, losing confidence and becoming very depressed until you gave him the encouragement he needed. As a result, you have one very staunch admirer and two very grateful parents.

Mentoring tip: Empathy includes making a genuine effort to understand the many physical, psychological, and social demands youth face.

Week 8

GOAL SETTING—A START

> Oxytocin is produced when we are trusted or shown a kindness and it motivates co-operation with others. It does this by enhancing the sense of empathy, our ability to experience others' emotions.
>
> —Paul Zak

DAY 1: THE ROLE OF THE GOAL GETTING MENTOR

When you encourage your mentees to set achievable goals their lives take on new purpose, and their energies are positively channeled in specific directions. Part of the goal-setting process during the mentoring journey is to assist your mentees to make sense of the confusion they may experience, which is normal at this stage of an adolescent's life.

Here are some ideas to think about as you guide your mentees on the goal getting journey.

- Identify and name their strengths.
- Identify their passions and interests.
- Determine how they respond to challenges. An important life experience for your mentee might be to learn, during their time with you, how to handle failure. Early in your mentoring relationship create an environment in which your mentee knows that failure is never fatal, but simply an important stepping-stone on the life journey. Share stories of people who have risked failure to achieve their dreams. Walt Disney and Thomas Edison are two well-known examples.
- Take non-life-threatening risks in a safe and secure environment.
- Plan, prioritize, and develop strategies which use resources available to them.

- Commit to something, and see it through to a conclusion.
- Identify and solve problems. Look at obstacles as opportunities to grow and develop.
- Guide and coach them how to evaluate their progress.
- Help them appreciate that they have control over their choices and goals most of the time.
- Help them appreciate that a dream is an end in itself, while goals are normally a means to an end. When all the goals or pieces of a puzzle come together, they will realize the dream.
- Coach them how to visualize their goals as if they have already achieved them. This increases their self-confidence and self-esteem.

Most of us have careers to think of, futures to secure, people to provide for, things to do. We need maps. We need direction. We need an itinerary. In other words, we need to set ourselves goals.

Mentoring tip: Great mentors encourage mentees to "begin" to imagine their futures, and help them shape and evaluate the course of their lives.

DAY 2: VOLUNTEER ADULT MENTORS AND GOALS

Here are some tips for mentors as they embark on a mentoring journey.

- You have a role as a coach and a cheerleader. Aim to motivate your mentee to move out of their comfort zone and maximize their potential.
- Your mentee looks to their parents and a range of other adults *in loco parentis*—mentors, teachers, workplace superiors—for definitions of life, goals, and values.
- Goal setting with your mentee requires patience, perseverance, encouragement, empathy, and being an exemplary role model.

Researchers have shared some positive outcomes of the effectiveness of goal getting strategies in a young person's life.

- Mentors observe a greater sense of pride and self-worth.
- A mentee gains increased knowledge and experience, especially when the focus is on topics of their interest.

- A mentee develops greater independence with regard to improving the ability to make choices.
- A mentee develops a stronger ability to respond to failures constructively and positively.
- A mentee develops a greater tolerance of calculated risk-taking.

Mentoring tip: Your role as a mentor is to inspire, motivate, and encourage your mentee to achieve realistic, achievable, measurable, and personally set goals.

DAY 3: WHY A MENTEE STRUGGLES TO SET GOALS

Someone once said that the instant you set a goal a light goes on in the future. I have seen this occur time and time again in the lives of adolescents I have mentored.

It might take time for a mentor to guide their mentee along the goal setting road. Be patient. Try to develop an understanding of some possible reasons for your mentee's reluctance to set goals. Here are a few common reasons.

- A fear of failure, criticism, or exposure, can be interwoven with a poor self-image.
- A poor self-image, which means they cannot see themselves achieving anything.
- A lack of an understanding of the benefits of goal setting.
- A lack of knowledge concerning how to develop a personalized, and effective goals program.
- Procrastination, which could be a sign of a rebellious spirit.
- Excuses, which could imply a refusal or unwillingness to assume responsibility, and be accountable for choices made.
- Laziness.
- Negative peer pressure, which is often a significant factor.
- A fear of success, which includes how to handle this success—for example, what further expectations would then be set when a goal is attained?
- A reluctance to move out of their comfort zone.

- A mentee is too busy with a range of activities, or possibly lives under an illusion of busyness, without any real focus or direction.

Mentoring tip: Coach your mentee that dreams turned into specific goals are a way to determine their personal success.

DAY 4: WRITE DOWN GOALS

One of the great conversations I have with youth occurs when they see no reason to write down their goals. "They are in my head," is a common response from the mentee.

The mentor's role is to coach their mentees how to set and achieve performance goals for the week, or month, or term (semester), and to visualize themselves achieving these goals.

- Mentees write down their goals—preferably on paper—to give them a clear understanding of what they need to do.

- Mentees break down their goals into small steps that are achievable and measurable. This, in turn, opens the way for them to evaluate their progress in a personal and ongoing way. Mentees become more enthusiastic, more confident, more competent, more courageous, and develop a positive self-image as they achieve their goals.

- Mentees write down their goals and then draw up schedules to achieve these goals. They train their developing brain. Activities like these help them manage their time and organize tasks—important employability skills—more effectively.

Mentoring tip: Mentoring involves showing that you care. Explore your mentee's dreams, goals and interests, and share a word of encouragement whenever you spend time together.

MENTORING MOMENTS

We often underestimate the power of mentoring and the impact it has on both the mentor and mentee's lives.

I believe that experiential mentor training significantly defines the success or otherwise of the mentoring relationship. Over the years I have trained over 1000 volunteer adult mentors. The interactions are always enjoyable, fun, challenging, and interesting as we exchange life experiences.

My motivation comes from the evaluations I receive at the conclusion of a twenty-one hours training course, held over seven weeks. I am always humbled and inspired to keep the training program relevant.

> "How useful and powerful the subject matter of the course. I believe that if the material in this course was taught not only to all parents who were struggling with parenthood, but also to the many, many adults who struggle with issues like self-esteem, self-belief, dealing with conflict, relationships, goal-setting, establishing direction and purpose in their life, and even establishing value sets, then society and its communities would be better off." (Adult participant)

> "Great course—wish I had been involved earlier! Quite aside from how this will assist with my mentoring process, 99 percent of it is transferable to my work situation—and life in general! Thank you. Reinforcement of themes is very effective. Very positive!" (Adult participant)

> "A wonderful self-awakening—especially enjoyed the thought of "the beauty inside" everyone and putting it into practice. Fast-tracked some of my personal goals. Affirmed to me the greatest gift is the gift of giving. Very enriching." (Adult participant)

> "A fantastic course of self-discovery. Should be open to everyone as a lot of people would learn about themselves and their actions." (Adult participant)

Mentoring tip: Always seek to be courageous, real, present, vulnerable, and responsive as you connect with youth.

Week 9

UNDERSTAND RESILIENCY

Children must be taught how to think, not what to think.
—Margaret Mead

DAY 1: RESILIENCY AND MENTORING

A significant outcome of a positive mentoring relationship is the development of a resilient young person.

Resilience is a process of "connectedness," as competent and emotionally stable mentors link to their mentees, their interests, and ultimately to life itself.

When you connect with your mentees, as you do when you nurture resiliency, you meet their emotional safety needs. While you cannot remove stress and adversity from their lives, you can provide them with the emotional safety which puts them in a position to develop problem solving and social skills. As the mentees develop these skills, along with competence in an area of their choice, they strengthen their self-confidence and sense of self-worth, identify and develop personal strengths, and gather the resources they need to stay strong when adversity threatens to overwhelm.

Research has found that mentees who connect with their mentor:

- are in a mutually caring, respectful mentoring relationship, in which the mentor encourages and nurtures the mentee's resilient qualities;
- have opportunities for meaningful involvement:
- they get along better with their parents, or caregivers, and teachers (authority figures);
- they develop a more positive attitude to life;
- they achieve more at school;

- they reduce their drug usage, alcohol abuse, truancy, and inappropriate sexual activities.

Mentoring tip: Seek to establish an emotional bond with your mentee and your relationship will soar.

DAY 2: IDENTIFY A MENTEE'S STRENGTHS

Personal resiliency builders are individual qualities that help people to cope with stress and adversity in their lives. One or more of these qualities can be identified in every adult and adolescent mentee. I think of them as strengths. Resiliency experts Nan Henderson and Sybil Wolin[1] have highlighted some of the most important personal resiliency builders.

Personal resiliency builder	**Definition**
Perceptiveness	Ask tough questions and give honest answers; have a perceptive understanding of people, and situations; display an insightful approach.
Relationships	Make fulfilling connections to other people; be sociable; able to be a friend, and form positive relationships.
Independence	Distance emotionally and physically from the sources of trouble in one's life; adaptive distancing from unhealthy people and situations; be autonomous, or self-sufficient.
Creativity	Use imagination and express oneself in art forms.
Humor	Have a good sense of humor; able to laugh at oneself.
Competence	Be personally "good at something"; have personal ability and skill in some area.
Initiative	Take charge of problems; base choices and decisions on internal evaluation (inner direction).
Perseverance	Keep on keeping on despite difficulty; never give up.
Flexibility	Able to adjust, or adapt to change; bend as necessary to cope positively with situations.
Love of learning	Have the capacity for and connection to learn; a desire to learn more.
Optimistic	Have a positive view of one's personal future; expect a positive future, or a positive outcome; be hopeful.
Self-worth	Feel self-confident; believe in oneself, and one's capabilities, even personal potential, and abilities.

1. Henderson, *Resiliency in Action*, 12.

Spirituality	Have a personal faith in something, or someone greater.

Mentoring tip: Turn every mentoring experience into a learning opportunity.

DAY 3: STRATEGIES TO DEVELOP RESILIENT MENTEES

Effective mentors have the responsible role to develop resilient mentees.

Here are some proven strategies to consider during the mentoring journey, all of which I have used at different times with a variety of adolescent mentees.

- Encourage your mentees to have diverse friendship groups and, wherever possible, to have at least one circle of friends outside of their school, workplace, or training institution.
- Encourage your mentees to join a youth club, sports club, or another club that caters for their interests.
- Encourage your mentees to link up with another caring, trustworthy adult from outside the immediate family, or extended family who they respect—a teacher, youth leader, work colleague, or sports coach.
- Encourage and coach your mentees to appreciate how thoughts influence feelings and behavior. In other words, nurture problem solving skills. Your mentees recognize that their conditional thinking—*You're stupid, or too thin, or a loser*—is a lie. They remove blocks to their innate resilience as they learn how to build their sense of competency in this way.
- Encourage your mentees to read, as cognitive competence has been identified as a hallmark of resiliency.
- Encourage your mentees to develop a close relationship with at least one parent (preferably both) where there is tension between parents—divorce, or separation.
- Encourage your mentees to contribute to daily life at home, for example by doing household chores, babysitting, or helping siblings.
- Encourage your mentees to be accountable for their choices. Demonstrate the importance of responsibility, and include your mentees in decision making, goal getting, and boundary setting.

Nourish your own resilience and wellbeing, so you can be an exemplary role model at all times.

Mentoring tip: A reliable and consistent mentor commits for the long haul.

DAY 4: THE UNIVERSAL CAPACITY FOR RESILIENCY

Resiliency expert Tony Newman[2] wrote: "A resilient young person can resist adversity, cope with uncertainty, and recover more successfully from traumatic events or episodes."

Everyone has strengths and an inborn capacity for self-righting, for transformation and change.

Bonnie Benard[3], one of the foremost authorities on resiliency in the world, has pointed out that all people are born with innate resiliency. That is, everyone has the capacity to develop four traits which are common among resilient survivors.

1. *Social competence*—the ability to form relationships, which includes responsiveness, cultural flexibility, empathy, caring, communication skills, and a sense of humor.
2. *Metacognition*—the ability to solve problems, which includes planning, help-seeking, and critical and creative thinking.
3. *Autonomy*—the ability to develop a sense of identity, self-efficacy, self-awareness, task mastery, and adaptive distancing from negative messages and conditions.
4. *A sense of purpose* and belief in a bright future—the ability to plan and hope, which includes goal direction, educational aspirations, optimism, faith, and spiritual connectedness.

Resilience is unlikely where a young person faces continuous and extreme adversity, which is not moderated by external factors. Conversely, the presence of a nurturing climate draws out the above traits and encourages their expression.

The link to nurturing is good news for mentors. It allows you to enter a mentoring relationship with the knowledge that, when you connect with your mentee, the two of you journey forward together with an optimistic

---

2. Newman, *Promoting Resilience.*
3. Benard, *Fostering Resiliency.*

and motivating attitude. "You" have the power to tip the scales from risk to resilience.

Mentoring tip: Effective mentors are encouragers and non-judgmental cheerleaders, not critics.

MENTORING MOMENTS

Pieter van der Bijl was my junior school principal. He was a former international cricketer who was highly respected by the students. He was a tall, imposing man who walked with a limp as a result of an injury he sustained in the North African campaign during the second World War.

Pieter wrote to my father before one of my major cancer operations to let him know that our family was in his thoughts and prayers. During my recovery, I missed a few months of school, yet Pieter continued to check up on my wellbeing.

One Saturday morning he arrived at our home to collect me and take me to watch school sport. Two of my peers accompanied him. We remained in the car to watch the sport, as it was a cold, wet and overcast day, and Pieter knew I was self-conscious as a result of my surgery.

Pieter was caring, compassionate, empathetic, and a wonderful encouragement. For a young boy recovering from major operations, it was comforting to know that my school principal watched over me, not only at that time, but also in the years that followed.

When I was appointed school captain (head student) for my final year of school, I received a letter from Pieter congratulating me on my achievements. He had retired by then and, sadly died a year later. Pieter's letter remains a treasured memoir from a man I respected and admired, and who sowed the seeds of mentoring in my life at a young age. I suspected, too, that he continually spoke to the potential he saw in me, which I did not see for quite some time after my surgery.

Mentoring tip: Always strive to build up youth with whom you connect. Encourage, correct, stretch, and sustain them every step of your mentoring journey.

Week 10

COMMUNICATION

The mediocre teacher tells. The good teacher explains. The superior teacher demonstrates. The great teacher inspires.

—William Arthur Ward

DAY 1: STAGES OF THE MENTORING RELATIONSHIP

There are three key stages in a mentoring relationship between a volunteer adult mentor and an adolescent mentee:

Stage 1: Get to know each other. This includes setting the boundaries for the relationship, planning meeting times, and building foundations of trust and respect. Be an encourager. Be the non-judgmental, affirming cheerleader your mentee will welcome into their life. You are the person who authentically says: "I believe in you!" and, "I know you can do this!," or, "I can see you achieving that! You are amazing!"

Stage 2: Focus on embarking on a goal setting and goal getting journey, while you maintain an element of fun. Celebrate small victories. Form a closer emotional bond with your mentee, and encourage them to develop meaningful relationships with other significant adults.

Stage 3: If your personal situation changes, or you are linked to a youth mentoring program, the third stage is to prepare your mentee for the official closure of the mentoring relationship. Where possible, help your mentee plan for the future, acknowledge the positive effects of the goal setting process, review and reflect on the high and low points of the relationship, and discuss options for how you can stay in touch in the future. Make sure you enjoy a special time to celebrate the mentoring journey.

Mentoring tip: Patience and perseverance are two key qualities to establish a positive connection with your mentee.

DAY 2: FIVE LEVELS OF COMMUNICATION

Various research findings suggest that there are possibly five different levels of communication a mentor passes through to establish a deeper, more meaningful, and trustworthy relationship with a mentee. Consider each of these levels, or stages.

1. *Cliches*: "How are you?"; "Where do you live?" These are general and non-threatening questions.
2. *Facts*: "Which film did you see?"; "What subjects do you enjoy?" These questions remain at a non-threatening level.
3. *Ideas*: "What do you think about that film or song?" "How valuable do you think that subject is to your career prospects?" These questions steer conversations to a deeper level.
4. *Feelings*: "How did you feel when you did not achieve that goal?"; "How did you feel when you were left out of the team last week?" Now our mentee moves into an area where they learn to be vulnerable.
5. *Intimate sharing*: "What was in your heart when your mum and dad told you they were separating?"; "What was going through your mind and heart when Jason decided to end the relationship?"

During the mentoring journey, you move from the surface responses at the lower levels, to ultimate sharing and connection with your mentee. Be patient, as this journey takes time for youth to share feelings and more intimate thoughts honestly. As a general rule, this is more prevalent with boys than with girls.

Arriving at the deeper levels depends on the length of the mentoring relationship, and the mentee's previous experiences of relationships with adults.

Some relationships might never reach the "intimate sharing" stage. This is no reflection on the mentor. The mentee chooses if and when they are ready to share at the deepest level.

Mentoring tip: Sometimes mentoring is a healing process, as you coach your mentee to trust again, and to remember that the sun shines after the storm has passed.

DAY 3: A GREAT LISTENER!

How well I remember the day seventeen-year-old Tracey sat in my office ranting about how unfair life was, how some of her teachers treated her unfairly, while they displayed special favor to others. On and on she went. Then she suddenly paused, looked at me, and said, "Why are you not saying anything?"

"I am listening," I quietly replied, and looked her in the eyes. She visibly relaxed, half-smiled, and apologized for her outburst.

"There's no need to apologize," I reassured Tracey. "Let's start looking for some solutions."

I remember showing her a large diagram of the brain. I explained to her what occurred in her brain when she had an emotional outburst such as I had just witnessed. We discussed new strategies to help her cope with similar situations, which would inevitably occur again. I can confidently say that a more skilled young person left my office that day. I know she worked hard to implement these strategies with a fair degree of success in the months ahead.

Mediator and trainer Nancy J. Foster stated that good communication skills are mutual respect skills. She believes that in the ideal world each person will show respect for the other as well as respect for themselves. This respect is displayed when we listen carefully to the other person. We seek clarification which shows how we "get" what that person is saying. We respect ourselves, yet unashamedly assert ourselves when we "give" our own legitimate self-interest without aggression. Foster suggested that when both people "get" and "give" a complete communication process occurs.

Mentoring tip: Listen! Listen! Listen with patience, an open mind, and be prepared to see the world through your mentee's eyes.

DAY 4: THE IMPORTANCE OF GOOD COMMUNICATION SKILLS

Clinical professor of psychiatry and author Daniel J Siegel[1] states: "Studies of the brain clearly show that reflection, inward or in communication with others, stimulates the activation and development of the prefrontal cortex [of the brain] towards its integrative growth."

Mentees enhance their self-confidence and develop meaningful relationships with others when they develop good communication skills.

---

1. Siegel, *Brainstorm*, 209.

Effective or active listening lies at the heart of mentoring. When mentees feel their mentors listen to them, they enjoy a positive growth mindset.

- They feel accepted as young people.
- They feel good about the mentor (the listener).
- They gain clarity about what has been on their mind.
- They think better about possible solutions.
- They feel less anxious (if they had been anxious).
- They receive a complete and accurate message.

Effective communication techniques are communication methods that help mentees talk and share their feelings and experiences in a place of safety and security.

Mentoring tip: When you have taught your mentee the skill of how to ask for help, you have shared a crucial life skill.

MENTORING MOMENTS

Fifteen-year-old Maya experienced learning difficulties at school. She thanked her mentor at the end of a nine-month school-based mentoring program.

> I'd just like to really say I think you are a great person. You care a lot about other people and have heaps of empathy. And you know, you are so wonderful to listen to, you always have something to say, or a joke to make, which is fantastic. I really admire you. I'd also like to say thanks for all the times you came and saw me at school, and something I was thinking about then, is how, whenever you would talk about your family, your children, it kind of gave me more of an understanding about how my mum might feel in a lot of situations. I mean, all you did was talk about your family, but it really has helped me in a way, so thank you.

Mentoring tip: Building meaningful relationships and connecting with youth involves opening your heart, and inviting them to share your life—a fun adventure.

Week 11

GOAL SETTING—THE PROCESS

> Building a bridge requires the help of other people. It is an active process involving connections, bonding, and collaboration; working together, we build a newer and richer mutual understanding.
>
> —Lisa Fain

DAY 1: SET ACADEMIC OR TRAINING GOALS WITH A MENTEE

One of the areas of performance goal setting I work through with adolescent mentees is linked to their education journey.

Not all mentees are academically inclined, yet they require academic foundations on which they can build the rest of their lives.

Look at your mentee's work over the previous year (or the previous term, or semester, depending on when the mentoring journey begins), and refer to records such as academic reports, for example, to gain a sense of your mentee's ability.

Use the information on academic ability to help your mentee set their realistic goals. If the mentee achieves their goals or, better still, surpasses them, their self-image improves, which has flow-on effects to other areas of life. If your mentee makes noticeable progress without reaching a goal, that remains a positive step forward, which you can acknowledge. Focus specifically on your mentee's *efforts*.

Remember that individuals differ in the pathway that works best for them. Many adolescents acknowledge that once their school grades improve, they achieve in many other areas. However, for some youth the starting point may be a noticeable advance in sport, or cultural pursuits, with the spin-off then seen in other areas of their lives (including academic achievement).

Once your mentee envisions a possible career, goal setting is easier. Encourage your mentee to explore possible careers. You are an important resource in this area. For example, you can introduce your mentee to people in careers that interest them.

If your mentee is involved in an apprenticeship, or some other form of practical training, encourage and guide them on how to set personal, realistic, and achievable goals, such as arriving on time at work, or at the training program, completing projects, or meeting specific program requirements.

Mentoring tip: A positive mentoring relationship results in your mentee's self-worth and academic achievements soaring.

DAY 2: SET FITNESS AND HEALTH GOALS WITH A MENTEE

One of the areas of performance goal setting I work through with youth is linked to their physical fitness and general health.

- Encourage some form of exercise. According to research, everyone should have "at least" thirty minutes of exercise every second day.
- What does your mentee enjoy doing, or wish to attempt? For example, they can join a gym, or undertake power walking, skateboarding, cycling, running, netball, volleyball, or basketball.
- Encourage your mentee to find out more information about positive role models in the activities with which they identify. What tips can your mentee pick up from their research on these people?
- Does your mentee eat a healthy breakfast every day? Does your mentee eat a healthy lunch if at work or attending an education institution? A balanced diet is important.
- Encourage your mentee to record daily exercise at the back of a diary. This task is excellent to develop a positive self-image. For example, your mentee shows you the diary at a monthly meeting with all exercise recorded. Wow! What a great opportunity for some positive affirmation.
- Encourage your mentee to join an exercise program with a friend, wherever possible, to reduce potential problems arising from negative peer pressure.

- Is there a teacher, a work colleague, or another adult who could help your mentee develop a suitable exercise program? Also, share *your* exercise program with your mentee and, in this way, you provide added motivation.

Mentoring tip: Never stop encouraging your mentee to develop and strive to achieve positive and lifelong goals.

DAY 3: SET EXTRACURRICULAR OR AFTER-WORK GOALS WITH A MENTEE

One of the areas of performance goal setting I work through with youth is linked to their social and cultural pursuits. Put another way, look at hobbies and interests, and make sure your mentee has a positive social life.

- What are your mentee's interests? Perhaps art, music, reading, computers, debating, photography, or skateboarding, or another sport? Obtaining a driver's license? Participation in a school drama, dance, debating, robotics, or music group, or another cultural activity? What opportunities are open to your mentee to explore these interests? For example, could your mentee join a local club, or youth group, or visit museums, art galleries, or cultural venues?
- As with exercise goals, your mentee can find out more about role models in their areas of interest. Is it possible to meet one of them, or watch a relevant YouTube clip together?
- Focus on one or two of these areas of interest every three to six months, and see what can be achieved.
- On occasion, after exploring an area of possible interest, your mentee may discover that they are not really interested in this particular activity. That is fine. Validate your mentee for exploring these new fields, and move on.
- How can you help your mentee? For example, could you visit exhibitions or the local library, or introduce your mentee to someone in a career of interest?
- Is there a teacher, a work colleague, or another adult who your mentee can speak to about a specific interest?

Mentoring tip: Great mentors "always" show up with messages of "hope" to encourage mentees to fulfill their potential.

DAY 4: SET FAMILY AND RELATIONSHIP GOALS WITH A MENTEE

One of the areas that could become a topic for performance goal setting with mentees relates to family relationships. You will discern how this can become a discussion topic when you form a trusting relationship with your mentee.

Here are some questions to encourage discussion about family relationships.

- What areas can your mentee work on to improve family relationships?
- What can your mentee contribute in this area? What tasks could your mentee do, such as child-minding, or watching over a grandparent from time to time, cooking, ironing, washing the car, taking the dog for a walk, or weeding the garden?
- How is communication between your mentee and their parents, or caregivers? Could they share goals and interests? Handle this area "sensitively."
- If your mentee is responsible for their accommodation, what goals can you set together in relation to areas such as washing dishes, clothes, tidying up, and maintaining a budget?
- How are your mentee's relationships with friends? How could they be improved? Your mentee will find friends everywhere when they chose to go through life with the intention of being a friend.
- Who are your mentee's closest friends? Why? Are they positive influences? Could your mentee introduce you to them? Could you do something together?

Mentoring tip: The positive involvement of your mentee's parents or caregivers in the mentoring journey enhances the mentoring partnership.

MENTORING MOMENTS

I have always gained immense satisfaction mentoring youth. I wear a variety of hats, dependent on the mentee's situation: teacher, coach, advocate, or volunteer mentor.

Often, I have no idea how much the interaction I have with a mentee impacts on their life. Imagine my surprise when I received this note from

Chris, with whom I had worked as a sport coach for about twelve months, and also taught for two years.

> ... how then was it that this very same team rose above all expectations, emerging as the top cricket school in [our state]? I believe the credit should be taken by a great cricketer, yet above and beyond that, a man adept enough in the teaching of life; those lessons in success, in character, in duty, in sportsmanship, and in camaraderie, to communicate it to schoolboys and get them to understand more about the game and themselves ... Perhaps this letter should be a more personal thank you, though, for the greatest lessons I ever learn in the "all round" education that [the school] offers. You taught me captaincy, you gave me motivation, and you bred the courage I had to accept the rough decisions I had ... Finally, Mr Cox, and perhaps this was a feeling never shown, it was really good to have you as a friend, too, a man I respected so highly.

Mentoring tip: You are most likely to connect and build meaningful relationships when youth feel valued and worth your time and effort.

Week 12

SELF-IMAGE

One can never consent to creep when one feels an impulse to soar.
—Helen Keller

DAY 1: FIVE KEY SIGNS OF A POSITIVE SELF-IMAGE

Over the years as I mentor youth, I assess the effectiveness of my mentoring journey with them. I consider if, most of the time, they reveal these five key signs of a positive self-image.

1. Mentees stand up to negative peer pressure, and appreciate that they are unique and special.
2. Mentees take acceptable risks that are not life-threatening, and appreciate their capabilities, and the importance of effort and performance.
3. Mentees risk moving out of their comfort zone as they learn to make sense and order out of the world with my support and encouragement—as well as with the support and encouragement of other significant adults in their lives.
4. Mentees handle mistakes and learn to appreciate that failure is okay as they strive to learn from such occurrences.
5. Mentees stick at tasks and goals until they have completed them. My role is that of the non-judgmental cheerleader.

Mentoring tip: Let your mentees explore the options available to define themselves. Create a safe, secure space for them to become the people they envision.

DAY 2: SIGNS OF SELF-IMAGE ISSUES

A mentee is on a journey through the most confusing time of their life, and their brain continues to develop until their mid-twenties. As a mentor gets to know their mentee, they observe patterns of behavior over an *extended period* of time, which *could* be a sign of a negative self-image, or low self-esteem.

Here are two examples:

Changes in performance

- deterioration in schoolwork;
- resistance to, or fear of new challenges;
- a tendency to put off doing tasks because they are bored, or the task is too hard;
- perfectionism;
- poor or no application to studies, rushing through work, messing around in class, and taking little pride in the end result;
- disorganization;
- no clear direction;
- no prioritizing;
- poor management of time;
- lack of interest in formerly precious things;
- loss of natural curiosity;
- reduction in study time;
- gives up easily—*I am a failure*, or *I am a loser*;
- missing the occasional sports practice, or arriving late.

Changes in social interaction

- begin to distance themselves from siblings, then from parents, then from other family members;
- shyness;
- seems too reserved;
- a loner at school, or in the workplace;

- friends stop telephoning, or texting, or visiting;
- clinginess;
- aggression;
- movement away from team sports or other team activities;
- difficulty forming lasting relationships;
- blaming others for their shortcomings, rather than taking responsibility.

Mentoring tip: Great mentors do not lose heart because of repeated disappointments and "never" quit on their mentees.

DAY 3: CAUSES OF A POOR SELF-IMAGE

There are many reasons why a mentee has a poor self-image. Some of the more common and challenging reasons are:

- a lack of "unconditional" parental love, which may be the greatest cause of an adolescent's poor self-image;
- alcohol abuse, or drug addiction in the family;
- parental divorce, or abandonment;
- a parent in prison, or other problems related to having only one parent;
- intolerable living conditions;
- parents who are on a welfare benefit;
- profane or immoral parents, who make it impossible to invite a friend home;
- the stigma that may be attached to living in foster care;
- experience of rejection or being made fun of by peers, leading mentees to believe that they are socially unacceptable and, consequently, that there is something wrong, or unpleasant, or undesirable about them;
- child abuse, which is one of the worst possible causes of a poor self-image.

Mentees will try out a variety of roles and personalities before they make more definitive decisions about their future goals. Their self-esteem is particularly fragile during this time. A mentor who accepts them unconditionally and takes on the role of an authentic, non-judgmental cheerleader, becomes an important influence in their lives.

Mentoring tip: Share thoughts with your mentees of what and who they can become. Express feelings of unconditional acceptance and affirmation.

DAY 4: WHY SELF-ESTEEM AND SELF-IMAGE ARE SIGNIFICANT IN ADOLESCENCE

Mentors appreciate that the development of a positive self-image and high self-esteem is important during adolescence. Generally, there are three key psychological tasks adolescents should accomplish:

1. Adolescents develop a sense of *personal identity* that consistently establishes who they are throughout each life role as a unique individual, separate and different from every other individual.

2. Adolescents begin the process of *establishing committed, intimate relationships*. The adolescent is asking key questions.

    - Who or what do I wish to be in life?
    - Where do I come from? (What is my family heritage?)
    - How do I look?
    - Will they like me?
    - Am I too pushy?
    - Will they think I am stuck up?
    - What judgments do I place on myself, and how do I feel about being me?
    - What decisions can I actually make and implement about my life and my future, and how much can I really control my environment?
    - What, if anything, is the value of being alive as a human?

3. Adolescents begin to make decisions that lead to *further training*, and entry into a particular *occupation or vocation*.

Whether or not an adolescent completes these three tasks successfully may determine much of what they subsequently accomplish, or fail to accomplish. The importance of your mentoring role in facilitating this life journey—as the wise guide—cannot be overemphasized.

SELF-IMAGE

Mentoring tip: Enhance your mentee's social skills and emotional wellbeing through your experiences together.

MENTORING MOMENTS

Fifteen-year-old Naomi, a participant in a school-based mentoring program, thanked her mentor Nora at the conclusion of the program. Naomi wrote:

> I just thought I would tell you how much fun I have had for the past semester or two and that I really appreciate you coming out of your way just to help me and to guide me so that I will not get lost. I am also looking forward to doing work experience with you. I am very grateful that you have taken the time to organize this. I just wanted to take the opportunity to say thank you. I am so excited!!!

Nora responded:

> I never thought at the beginning of our journey last year that today would be so happy and joyous. No need to apologize or feel bad that I was brought to tears today. They were happy tears, tears of joy and being so proud of the strong lady you are maturing into. The sky is the limit for you Naomi. Reach high and your family and I will be by your side all the way.

Nora and Naomi's relationship remains strong today, over fifteen years since the formal program ended.

Mentoring tip: Never stop reminding young people to turn obstacles into positive and life-changing opportunities.

Week 13

LOOKING AT CONFLICT

Failure is the opportunity to begin again more intelligently.
—Henry Ford

DAY 1: IDENTIFY A MENTEE'S CONFLICT STYLE (1)

Each person's conflict style is developed over time. It is a product of many factors, which probably include some, or all of the following:

- society's attitudes towards conflict, which we assimilated early on life's journey;
- our observations of how our parents, teachers, media heroes—TV stars, sports stars, pop stars, artists—and other significant role models deal with conflict;
- our personal experiences of conflict.

When we understand the three broad conflict styles, not only will this help us to understand ourselves better, but we can also understand a mentee's reaction to various conflict situations. These are three styles, briefly explored in the next three Mentoring Minutes messages.

1. Avoidance.
2. Confrontation.
3. Problem solving.

My observations over the years—during mentor training—are that many mentors have found the positive approach to resolving a conflict valuable, both with regard to their own personal development, as well as for the mentoring experience.

Mentoring tip: Move alongside your mentee during their darkest hours—an SMS, email or card could be life-changing for the young person.

DAY 2: IDENTIFY A MENTEE'S CONFLICT STYLE (2)

We approach conflicts in different ways. One of the most common styles is that of *avoidance*. Avoidance takes many subtle forms. The most common of these forms are "denial" and "accommodation." "Denial" of a conflict is likely to result in any, or all of the following reactions and outcomes:

- anger, frustration, hurt, and resentment;
- backbiting, or gossip;
- an escalation of conflict.

The basis of "accommodation" or "capitulation" is that it is easier to agree than to diagnose. It involves apologizing, finding reasons to justify differences in opinions, and adjusting one's opinion and behavior. The likely consequences are

- the avoidance of a threat to a friendship, as true feelings are not expressed;
- an escalation of conflict.

Peer pressure—which gains its power from the desire to have friends—may lead adolescents to choose "accommodation" as a realistic way to deal with conflicts. I remember choosing this style in my youth.

The key point in any discussion about resolving conflicts is to ask mentees how they can de-escalate a conflict. You might be surprised that, most times, young people know what needs to be done. All that is required is for someone to walk alongside them while they work through the issues.

Mentoring tip: Remind your mentees that you are there to help and encourage them to fulfill their hearts' desires.

DAY 3: IDENTIFY A MENTEE'S CONFLICT STYLE (3)

Where *confrontation* is the conflict style, a person deals with conflicts head-on. Specifically, the confrontational person

- sees conflict as a win–lose situation, and is determined to prove they are right; they may keep information hidden to achieve this end (so there might even be an element of dishonesty present);
- may increase the level of aggression, and express insults and threats;
- usually displays poor listening skills (as may the other party in the conflict).

A "confrontational" person tends to "use (and abuse) power." They often make threats based on authority or power. This behavior is common in relationships between older and younger siblings; parents and children; teachers and students, or employers and employees.

It is characterized by the use of "... because I said so!" in preference to discussion and negotiation and, in most cases, is likely to escalate conflict.

This conflict style is often expressed by mentees who have particular difficulties with authority figures. Coach them the meaning of empathy. Use examples, and never underestimate the power of such conversations to cause positive behavior changes.

Mentoring tip: Great mentors practice empathy with their mentees. They try to understand what the mentees share, and listen carefully to the feelings being expressed.

DAY 4: IDENTIFY A MENTEE'S CONFLICT STYLE (4)

A person is less concerned with who is "right" or "wrong," and more concerned to find a solution that will be satisfactory to both parties when *problem solving* is the style used to resolve a conflict. The main methods to reach this end are "compromise" and "collaboration."

For "compromise," each person involved

- must give up something;
- wins partially, and loses partially.

If a person must let go of something they value, simply for the sake of compromise, this form of conflict resolution could lead to unhappiness and resentment. Perhaps in such cases, compromise becomes another form of "accommodation," and the conflict could escalate.

Where "collaboration" is used to resolve a conflict, the people involved

- explore how to meet each other's needs;

- seek a win–win solution where neither person loses;
- need to understand the conflict's cause, and what is at stake for the other person;
- need to commit themselves to a process that takes time, perseverance, and skill;
- agree to a follow-up meeting to make sure both parties are comfortable with the process.

Mentoring tip: As you reach out to shape and influence your mentee's life, two lives are positively enriched—yours and your mentee's.

MENTORING MOMENTS

I was about eleven years of age when Herby Selfe called me aside.

After school many students would gather on the small field, and kick a ball, or play other games. One winter's afternoon I was playing football. Herby called across to me: "Coxy!"—first names were not used in those days. Herby had been marking exam papers. I forget which subject it was.

We sat on the steps of the old farmhouse, which housed the art room, other classrooms, changing rooms, and the staff room.

I was confident I had performed well in the exam. How wrong I was. I had failed. For about thirty minutes Herby went through the paper with me, and pointed out careless error after careless error.

I was still recovering from cancer operations, and the recent death of my mother. Herby knew all this.

I have never forgotten that day when Herby sat with me. At no time did he pass judgment. I felt care and compassion, and heard a teacher tell me that he had more confidence in my ability than I truly appreciated. He cared about me and my future.

From that time on, throughout my school career, and in the years after school, Herby and I always stopped for a chat when our paths crossed. I felt like we had an unspoken bond between us. Herby modeled the spirit of mentoring in my life for many years, and became a trustworthy, and highly respected friend.

Mentoring tip: Continually remind yourself that it requires patience, persistence, and time to connect, and develop meaningful relationships with youth.

Week 14

MENTORING REFLECTIONS

There are only two lasting bequests we can hope to give our children. One of these is roots, the other, wings.

—Hodding Carter

DAY 1: THE MENTOR AS A FRIEND

As friendship is at the core of your relationship with your mentee, consider some important character qualities you can continually develop to enjoy a meaningful and effective relationship with your mentee.

Be *Fun*-loving	Have lots of fun together. Nurture a sense of humor. Model what it means to laugh at yourself.
Be *Respectful**	Respect both your mentee and yourself as unique beings of great self-worth with a positive self-image. Acknowledge the right of your mentee to make personal choices.
Be a person of *Integrity*	Be honest and truthful at all times. Be consistent and show up on time. Be upright and reliable. Be committed to the relationship. Be someone your mentee can depend on. Be authentic.
Be *Empathetic**	Place yourself in the shoes of your mentee to the best of your ability in order to understand them better. Your understanding helps you inspire a young person to greatness.
Be *Nurturing*	Create a supportive relationship in which your mentee feels cared for, affirmed, and encouraged. Key features in establishing this relationship include being an effective "listener," committing time to your mentee, believing in them, being accessible to them, and giving of yourself unconditionally to this relationship.

Be *D*evelopmental in your thinking	Encourage your mentee to become the person they wish to be. This is a process that takes time and requires patience, perseverance, and the understanding that a friendship takes time to develop. No "saviors" or "quick fixes" are needed.
Be Sincere*	Be yourself at "all" times. Be genuine. That is, be aware of your innermost thoughts and feelings, accept them and, when appropriate, share them responsibly. Model a spirit of the servant mentor.

* = These are key qualities, or foundation stones of meaningful relationships.

Mentoring tip: Effective mentors nurture and encourage a positive growth mindset.

DAY 2: ADOLESCENT CHALLENGES

There are real challenges facing adolescents between the ages of eleven and nineteen. This highlights the important role a mentor or other significant adult plays in that young life. Here are some challenges youth confront.

- A child deprived of unconditional love in the development years is often unable to relate effectively to others, or to love themselves.
- A child who has not received love frequently finds it difficult to give love.
- Children who do not feel valued often do not value themselves or others.
- The adolescent years involve testing new beliefs, new systems, new ways of operating and behaving, and finding out what other ways of life are like. It is better to experiment with and discover through these experiences within the safety and security of family, or extended family structures.
- Mentees must gain opportunities to face the consequences of their behavior if they are to become responsible young people. Policy analyst and author, Jennifer Buckingham[1] stated:

  > The child with a strong, affectionate family, whose parents care for his or her welfare, and supervise his or her behavior and schooling, is more likely to be successful at school, less likely to become suicidal, and less likely to fall into delinquency and juvenile crime. Such a family is a protective and positive factor in every sense.

1. Buckingham, *Boy troubles*.

Mentoring tip: Positively involve your mentee's parents or caregivers in the mentoring journey as best as you can.

DAY 3: THE VALUE OF A CARING ADULT

A few years ago, I read an interesting document written by the United States Department of Education[2]. The document pointed out the significant value of a sustained presence of a caring adult in a mentee's life. It highlighted how critical this is as students made potentially life-changing decisions about what academic courses to take, what activities to participate in, and how seriously they would approach their education challenges.

Who should these mentors be? What qualities should they have?

Here are some suggestions the authors shared.

- Demonstrate commitment, competence, and a willingness to extend knowledge.
- Derive satisfaction from helping others succeed.
- Be a role model, advisor, and friend.
- Build confidence by teaching skills, and offering feedback.
- Exhibit ethical behavior.

Mentoring tip: Teach your mentees how to step back from their problems to live a stress-less life.

DAY 4: DISCUSSION TOPICS WITH MENTEES

Mentors often ask me what topics they should talk about, especially during the early days of the mentoring partnership.

Every mentoring relationship is different. Some mentors connect with their mentees almost immediately, while others take up to six months—even longer—for this connection to occur.

Here are some safe, non-threatening and proven topics, which I have found helpful.

- What are your expectations of this mentoring experience?
- What role would you like me to play as your mentor?
- In what ways can I help, or support you?

---

2. United States Education Department, *Yes You Can*, 28.

- How many people are in your family or extended family? Who do you get along with best? Why?

- Who do you admire—who is your hero—in the world? Who is someone you would enjoy being like, or would like to meet? Why? What qualities does that person have? I would like to know more about them, or maybe we could see if we can find out more information together.

- How do you spend your free time? What are your interests, or hobbies?

I came across this statement written by an unknown author. It encourages mentors to appreciate their importance in the life of a young person.

> Ensuring the sustained presence of a caring adult in a young person's life is especially critical during adolescence . . . [when] students face serious decisions about which courses they will take, what activities they will engage in, and how seriously they will take their schoolwork . . . For the most at-risk youth, the presence of an adult mentor can be essential for reinforcing the importance of school, fostering good work habits and study skills, and providing youth with the information they need to make the right choices.

Mentoring tip: Always make sure that your mentees are aware that you want them to grow and advance during the mentoring journey.

MENTORING MOMENTS

A group of seventeen-year-old girls who were training to become peer mentors shared the most important lessons they gained from the day's training. These responses reveal something about the thinking of adolescent girls and what might also be important to them.

> "To be non-judgmental; to listen and not interrupt; to be empathetic; not to talk down to the mentee; don't fix it unless it's something life threatening."

> "How to be a good listener; don't gossip or interrupt others while they are talking; take responsibility in what you are doing; summarize what you put together; repeat what your mentee has said so you understand."

> "Communication; understanding; opening up; always be the best you can be; we're role models."

"Setting goals; managing time; my facial expressions and actions when listening; it's not what I can get out of it, but for the mentee; it's not to give advice but to try and steer them in the right direction."

"I don't have to give advice and set directions to my mentee; that interaction and understanding will help me communicate better; that time management is important; that listening is important and it helps gain a stable friendship; being who I am and a role model is a good key!"

"Acceptance of others; appreciation of each other; listening goes further than expected; how vulnerable we all are; we are all the same, so should treat each other kindly."

"Being appreciative of others; making an effort to be more approachable; gaining trust—how to; some of these things will help me with an outside friend in need; becoming a better listener."

"Listen; it is not my responsibility if my mentee makes mistakes; there is help left, right and center; don't gossip; appreciate time. I am the influence."

Mentoring tip: Make sure young people always feel safe and secure in your presence. Then you can positively—yet sensitively, and empathetically—challenge and encourage them.

Week 15

ASSERTIVENESS

The mind is not a vessel to be filled, but a fire to be kindled.
—Plutarch

DAY 1: A CHECKLIST FOR ASSERTIVENESS

Assertive mentors model some key characteristics and qualities during the time they spend with their mentees. I am indebted to the work carried out by psychotherapist and self-help expert Gael Lindenfield[1] for much of this information.

Here are some assertive statements to think about.

- I have a positive outlook on life and on others. I am keen to impart unconditional love and care, and to encourage my mentee to *feel* like a winner.
- I have a realistic view of myself—*I am human*. I acknowledge my strengths and weaknesses, and know the limits of my strength and potential.
- I take responsibility for myself and my life. I don't blame others because of my situation, or emotional state. I admit my mistakes, and look after myself physically. I am a rock on which my mentee depends.
- I am an imaginative and creative thinker, and can be depended on to find new ways around seemingly impossible problems.
- I am versatile—a jack of all trades and master of setbacks. I am adaptable and avoid ruts.
- I am determined. I don't put myself down, as I believe in myself.

---

1. Lindenfield, *Success*.

- I have an inner sense of security, contentment, and humility. I want my mentee to grow and advance.
- I am well organized and efficient. I can weigh up options before I make decisions. I know how to set achievable goals, rather than set myself up for failure.

Mentoring tip: Always make your mentee feel like a champion. That is what a non-judgmental cheerleader does.

DAY 2: MENTORS ARE ASSERTIVE ROLE MODELS

During the mentoring journey we consider assertiveness as the ability to honestly stand up for yourself, your beliefs, your ideas, and your opinions—even when under stress—without violating someone else's rights using some form of power or manipulation.

For example, an assertive person expresses anger constructively, which will involve:

- an expression of anger in a way that is personal to themselves, rather than judgmental towards others;
- using *I* statements, rather than *You* statements.

You can positively influence your mentee by modeling this kind of assertive behavior. You play a key stabilizing and encouraging role during the mentoring journey with young people who experience significant change in many areas of their lives. Well-known Australian parenting expert, Steve Biddulph[2], wrote:

> Adolescence is the age of passion. Boys [and girls] crave an engaged and intense learning experience, with men and women who challenge them and get to know them personally—and from this specific knowledge of their needs, work with them to shape and extend their intellect, spirit, and skills. If kids aren't waking up in the morning saying, "Wow! School today!" then something is not right.

Mentoring tip: Mentors model positive attitudes and thinking, always in the role of the non-judgmental cheerleader.

---

2. Biddulph, *Raising Boys*.

ASSERTIVENESS

DAY 3: ENCOURAGE A MENTEE TO BE ASSERTIVE

There are many ways a mentor can encourage a mentee to develop assertiveness. Your mentee develops resiliency as you do this.

Here are a few proven strategies which I have used when mentoring youth (and adults).

- Help your mentee to feel valued as a unique individual. Ask them to help you with a task or activity.
- Affirm your mentee and make positive comments about their appearance, intelligence, and abilities. Reinforce the good qualities that make your mentee unique and special.
- Help your mentee to feel understood. Encourage them to express beliefs verbally and in writing without fear of being put down or judged.
- Expect the best from your mentee. This positive attitude assists the development of an *"I can!"* attitude when you deal with challenging issues.
- Catch, observe, and praise things your mentee does well, and always focus on their *effort*.
- Remind your mentee that it is not necessary to be perfect in order to feel loved and capable.
- It is okay for your mentee to experiment provided it does not pose any serious risk to life, health, or values.
- Encourage your mentee to make good choices, rather than allow others to make choices for them.
- Encourage your mentee to move out of their comfort zone with your support, and believe in them. This is often an amazing journey of self-discovery and empowerment.

Mentoring tip: Effective mentors affirm in public and correct in private.

DAY 4: NURTURE HIGH SELF-ESTEEM

As high self-esteem is essential for healthy living and the formation of meaningful relationships, here are some signs of high self-esteem mentors can look out for in their relationship with mentees.

- A sense of being comfortable with and positive about others.

- A sense of responsibility towards others, and an ability to love others and consider their interests; to respect and accept the differences they see in others, and to accept love and praise from others.
- An ability to understand, accept, and negotiate boundaries.
- An ability to find acceptable compromises without having to sacrifice their self-respect or integrity, or to exploit, or violate the rights of others.
- An enjoyment of their own company, and an appreciation of the value of time to reflect, rest, and renew energy.
- A feeling of uniqueness, inner worth, and confidence; an ability to laugh at themselves; an ability to understand how their body changes; possessing the insight to be in touch with their emotions, such as fear, anger, love, jealousy, and worry; a sense of being at peace with themselves and others; and a sense of feeling competent, capable, and lovable.
- Good organization skills.
- Good management of time skills.
- A sense of "connection" to family, school, work, and peers, and of being valued by others.
- A sense of "power" because they have the resources necessary to carry out their own purposes, and an ability to make decisions, solve problems, and handle pressure and stress.
- Emotional security, and a sense of freedom from physical harm.
- A belief that their lives have meaning and purpose.
- An interest in who they are, rather than with what they do.

Mentoring tip: A real, effective mentoring relationship of mind and heart enriches and sustains both parties.

MENTORING MOMENTS

There is that wonderful moment when, many years after I have mentored a student, our paths cross.

I am left humbled when I receive a comment such as this, written by Ross:

It is very nice to be in touch. I have always wanted to thank you for the role you played in my life at [school]. I remember our history lessons with pleasure, but mainly chats and a Coke after our weekly squash games. It made a big difference to me that you showed me that care and interest. I have appreciated that for thirty years, and think of you often. It is with you that I recall having my first conversation with anyone about wanting to become a [career choice] . . . It has gone well for me, but the first step was with you, and our discussions of why I lost matches from 2–0 up were my first [career] experiences. Mentoring Matters is a wonderful project that I am sure has given you the opportunity to affect many lives in the way you influenced mine.

Mentoring tip: Be an authentic and effective role model who builds character in young people with whom you interact.

Week 16

COMMUNICATION INFLUENCES

Advice is like snow; the softer it falls, the longer it dwells upon, and the deeper it sinks into the mind.

—Samuel Taylor Coleridge

DAY 1: WHAT INFLUENCES COMMUNICATION (1)

Here are some key points to influence positive communication experiences between a mentor and a mentee.

- We are unique individuals; each of us differs from all others. We come from different families, and possibly different ethnic backgrounds and cultures, and we have different personal experiences.
- We differ in the things we want from life and from each other.
- We differ in our dreams, wishes, and expectations.

Our uniqueness means that two individuals may respond in different ways to the same situation. This potentially complicates communication greatly. Communication is likely to be difficult dependent on how much two people (or groups of people) differ in values, perceptions, and assumptions.

As mentors, we continually remind ourselves of our role as a "non-judgmental cheerleader." It is a challenge, but worth striving to attain if we want to connect with our mentees, many of whom are at the age where they struggle to share their feelings and vulnerabilities.

William Arthur Ward wrote these wonderful words which continually inspire me to persist as a mentor when I feel frustrated, and want to quit: "Flatter me and I may not believe you. Criticize me and I may not like you. Ignore me, and I may not forgive you. Encourage me and I will not forget you."

Mentoring tip: You communicate your values with your mentee when you share your life experiences.

DAY 2: WHAT INFLUENCES COMMUNICATION —VALUES (2)

Values define who we are and inform our decisions about how we live our lives. Many clashes between adults and youth are caused by differences in their value systems in relation to issues such as age-appropriate videos or films, appropriate use of social media, drinking alcohol, smoking—or vaping—experimenting with drugs of any sort, and inappropriate sexual behavior.

Values are based on our beliefs about what is morally right and correct, what is important, and what is true.

Values also involve those beliefs we hold most dear, such as religious, social, and cultural beliefs.

A key point to remember in any mentoring relationship is that mentors should *never* impose their values on their mentees. Focus instead on becoming a positive role model.

Adolescents listen to everything adults say, even though at times they pretend they are not hearing anything. At about eighteen years of age, they begin to formulate the values—from their life experiences to date—they will start to live by. Educator and author Dr. Paul Browning[1] writes: "Good listeners look for the emotions a person is expressing. Great listeners look for what the person *values*. Values cut to the heart of identity. They define and control our actions."

Mentoring tip: Never be afraid to tell your mentees you disapprove of their behavior. Do not quit on them, or forget to display unconditional love and care.

DAY 3: WHAT INFLUENCES COMMUNICATION— PERCEPTIONS (3)

Two individuals can experience the same event or look at the same object, and perceive two entirely different events or experiences. Such differences in perception arise as each of us brings to every situation a mindset that shapes what we see and hear. This mindset is formed from our values, our previous experiences, our culture, and our expectations.

1. Browning, *Principled*, 28.

Teach your mentees how to look at a situation objectively as they consider all viewpoints. This assists the development of effective communication skills in a wide range of relationships.

Author Victor Orneles wrote: "What's important to appeal to teenagers is to be genuine. Teenagers are easily disillusioned by events and trends. They walk to their own beat."

Psychologist, education reformer, and entrepreneur Roger C. Shank offers an idea to develop values and perceptive thinking during the mentoring journey: "Story telling enhances people's emotional connectedness and understanding of concepts. It's also what the brain likes best."

When we share our life experiences—as mentors—we talk about how we perceived situations, and what we learnt from these experiences. Mentees listen with interest!

Mentoring tip: Effective mentors model the attitudes they would like their mentees to develop.

DAY 4: WHAT INFLUENCES COMMUNICATION— ASSUMPTIONS (4)

An assumption is a statement, or judgment that a person makes with an acceptance that it is true without proof or demonstration. For example, we make an assumption when we stereotype, or label others, or cast suspicion on others without having all the facts: "All teenagers abuse alcohol."

Assumptions about other people or situations spring from our values and perceptions. We assume or infer things about others based on what we believe and perceive.

Mentees are often angered when someone gives them a stereotypical label, or when adults especially draw conclusions about them based on assumptions, or even past behavior. Where these feelings are experienced by one of your mentees, you can work through them together and, in so doing, help your mentee develop constructive coping and tolerance skills.

At the same time, you coach mentees not to fall into the trap of stereotyping peers, teachers, and others with whom they interact on a regular basis.

Mentoring tip: Effective mentors follow a policy of "show and tell"—this is great modeling.

MENTORING MOMENTS

Why do people volunteer to mentor? How do they feel at the formal end of a nine-month school-based mentoring program?

Here are some comments from mentors of fifteen-year-old students who had a further two years at school after the completion of the mentoring program.

> "[My mentee] began the program wanting to leave school at the end of the year and lacking in confidence. She now believes there are a lot of opportunities out there suited to her talents and is keen to go on to complete her schooling."

> "We discussed training options for going into child care and, based on what I knew about her, I was able to direct her into a way that would get her to achieve her goal. I enjoyed the program overall."

> "We widened the range of possibilities for future studies and careers. Initially he was only looking at paramedics, but is also now looking at business studies as an alternative. I think the program is a wonderful initiative . . ."

> "Helped keep him moving forward . . . support from staff was excellent and [I enjoyed] the freedom within the program scope to find the path that best suited the mentee."

> "I do believe I have helped him become a bit more focused on what and where he wants to go with his life."

> "Perhaps the ground work was put down for future mentoring."

Mentoring tip: Coach and guide youth how to turn every crisis into a new opportunity.

Week 17

SIX STEP CONFLICT RESOLUTION PROCESS

A leader takes people where they want to go. A great leader takes people where they don't necessarily want to go, but ought to be.

—ROSALYNN CARTER

DAY 1: A SIX-STEP PROCESS TO POSITIVELY RESOLVE CONFLICTS (1)

I have learnt over the years, as I work with mentees to resolve conflicts, that they have the ability to share these skills within their own family, and with their peers.

If appropriate to your mentee's particular situation, talk through the six-step process together. The next three Mentoring Minutes messages briefly outline each step. The process is helpful to your mentee as they work to resolve a conflict, and learn how to approach it with a positive, rather than a negative mindset.

Share with your mentee that a general principle to follow when they deal with a conflict, is, wherever possible, to "take the initiative," and approach the other party as soon as they can. Ask the other person for an opportunity to restore the relationship, or to discuss their differences.

If this approach is rejected, they can leave the door open for future discussion and, tough though it may be sometimes, they should try and move on with their lives. It is invaluable to discuss these moments with a mentor, or another trustworthy adult.

If this approach is accepted, work through the following six steps with your mentee.

1. Plan ahead and analyze.

2. Set the tone for the meeting.
3. Discuss and define the problem.
4. Summarize the new understanding.
5. Brainstorm alternative solutions.
6. Follow-up.

Mentoring tip: A mentor shares life lessons they have picked up when they worked through conflict situations. Their mentees will listen with interest.

DAY 2: A SIX-STEP PROCESS TO POSITIVELY RESOLVE CONFLICTS (2)

In the previous message, we moved to a point where both parties have agreed to meet and resolve the conflict.

Step 1 (of the six-step process to positively resolve conflicts): *Plan ahead and analyze.* Consider these questions as you prepare for your meeting:

- What specifically concerns me about this conflict?
- How does it affect me?
- Why is it important to me? What are my values?
- What would make the situation better for me?

Step 2: *Set the tone for the meeting.* You can establish a constructive tone at the outset.

- State positive intentions. For example: "I want this issue to be resolved"; "I value this friendship"; "I really want to understand this."
- Acknowledge, validate, and affirm the other person. For example: "I appreciate your willingness to talk about this"; "Thank you for this opportunity to chat"; "I can see that you are also taking this matter seriously." Authenticity is important throughout the conflict resolution process.

Mentoring tip: When you decide to share your time, your gifts, your life experiences and your trust with your mentee, you give an invaluable gift of yourself.

DAY 3: A SIX-STEP PROCESS TO POSITIVELY RESOLVE CONFLICTS (3)

In the previous message, we considered the first two steps of the six-step process to positively resolve conflicts. Here are the next two steps.

Step 3: *Discuss and define the problem.* Each person expresses their issues and feelings honestly, assertively, and sensitively. For example, one person expresses their issues and feelings, while the other listens carefully to make sure they understand what is being shared.

- Use your ears more than your mouth, as you must first attempt to empathize with the other person's feelings.
- Use effective communication techniques and guides. Even if you do not agree with everything the other person says, allow them to unload emotionally without becoming defensive. The message you convey will be: *I am listening. I value your opinion. I care about our relationship. You matter to me.*
- Identify interests and needs.
- Discuss any assumptions, suspicions, and values where necessary. If you know you have made mistakes, humbly admit them, apologize, and ask for forgiveness.

Step 4: *Summarize the new understanding* that you have reached with the other person.

- Reflect and restate where necessary to ensure full clarification.
- Choose your words wisely, and deal with the root cause, or causes of the problem, rather than judge the other person.

You are ready to brainstorm solutions, which is covered in the next Mentoring Minutes message.

Mentoring tip: Encourage your mentee to accept the costs and consequences of choices. Inspire positive choices.

DAY 4: A SIX-STEP PROCESS TO POSITIVELY RESOLVE CONFLICTS (4)

In previous messages, we looked at the first four steps of the six-step process to positively resolve conflicts. Here are the final two steps.

SIX STEP CONFLICT RESOLUTION PROCESS

It is time to seek a solution to the conflict, as you are now in a position to agree on the best options.

Step 5: *Brainstorm alternative solutions.*

- Determine the advantages and disadvantages of each course of action; consider consequences, and do a reality check.
- Choose solutions that are mutually acceptable. Make sure the solutions are specific and balanced; win–win is the first prize.
- Do your best to compromise, especially when collaboration is difficult. Adjust to the needs and preferences of the other person if you can genuinely do so.

Step 6: *Follow-up.* Agree on a time in the very near future (about a week at the most) and a place, or method, such as a call or email—preferably a face-to-face meeting—to assess progress. *This key area of follow-up is often ignored or overlooked in the process to positively resolve a conflict.*

Even at the end of the conflict resolution process you might not have reached agreement on everything. If the relationship is important to you remember that reconciliation is sometimes the way towards resolution of a problem. You can agree to disagree, and from there re-establish a relationship.

Mentoring tip: Guide your mentee towards honesty and always model integrity and truth.

MENTORING MOMENTS

I was sixteen years of age when I met Mike Denness on a beautiful summer's afternoon in Cape Town. I was about to make my first cricket team debut, and stood on the boundary probably soaking up the possibilities instead of focusing on the practice.

Mike Denness had arrived that day from England, where he was a professional cricketer. He would coach us for the season.

I heard a broad Scottish accent behind me gently, yet firmly, chiding me for my sloppy attitude. My cricket life changed from that moment on.

I was young and wanted to impress my coach, so I responded to the challenge. More important, though, were the face to face conversations I had with Mike. He shared his experiences and coached me how to approach the game, talked about attitude, and how to develop a competitive approach while always playing the game in the right spirit, the importance of teamwork, and never to give up.

Mike taught me much about life, sport, and myself during an important season of my life, as I began to spread the wings of independence. I was like a sponge soaking up all these experiences. I thanked Mike on his departure for the profound impact he had on my life as a coach and friend. Two years later he was selected as captain of England.

Mentoring tip: Always seek to celebrate the growth, efforts, and achievements of youth.

Week 18

FEATURES OF ADOLESCENTS AGED BETWEEN THIRTEEN AND FIFTEEN

Tell me and I forget, teach me and I may remember, involve me and I learn.

—BENJAMIN FRANKLIN

DAY 1: FEATURES OF ADOLESCENTS AGED BETWEEN THIRTEEN AND FIFTEEN (1)

In the period between thirteen and fifteen years of age, adolescents *move from dependence through interdependence towards independence.* The majority of young people in this age group deal with challenges like those mentioned below, as their brains continue to develop—they

- struggle with a sense of identity;
- feel awkward or strange about their self or body;
- focus on self, often alternating between high expectations and a poor self-concept;
- have interests and clothing styles that are influenced by the peer group;
- are moody and behave in unpredictable ways;
- develop their ability to express themselves verbally;
- come to realize that parents are not perfect. As they begin to identify their parents' faults, conflict with their parents increases;
- show less overt affection to parents, and are occasionally rude to them;
- spend more time with peers;
- complain that parents interfere with their independence;

- tend to return to childish behavior, particularly when stressed;
- become part of cliques with similar values;
- begin to assert their value systems, which are a work in progress for the next few years;
- day-dream;
- are more likely to conform to peer pressure;
- do not want to go to school for reasons such as depression, anxiety about academic performance, perfectionism, social worries, and hopelessness about school. These are feelings that can be created across all age groups by traumatic death, loss or injury, parental illness, or family problems.

Mentoring tip: Listen for feelings. Remember that young people often hide their true feelings from adults and peers in case they are rejected.

DAY 2: FEATURES OF ADOLESCENTS AGED BETWEEN THIRTEEN AND FIFTEEN (2)

Here are some comments about youth between the ages of thirteen and fifteen to enhance the quality of a mentoring relationship. Generally, youth

- are most interested in the present, with limited thoughts of the future;
- are expanding and giving more priority to their intellectual interests;
- are more able to do work requiring physical, mental, and emotional energy;
- begin to solve problems by considering alternatives;
- become more self-conscious and self-focused;
- are only starting to evaluate vocational options in terms of interests.

Here are some scenarios involving normal adolescent behavior to help you understand your mentee and the challenges being faced.

- Mentees are confused and disinterested in the future.
- Mentees are secretive.
- Mentees are argumentative.
- Mentees are angry when interrogated.

- Mentees resent personal questions.
- Mentees are uncommunicative.

Mentoring tip: Great mentors "always" genuinely respect their mentee's viewpoint and opinions—you might be the only person in their life doing so.

DAY 3: FEATURES OF ADOLESCENTS AGED BETWEEN THIRTEEN AND FIFTEEN (3)

It is helpful for mentors to reflect on the findings of research with regard to sexuality features of adolescents aged between thirteen and fifteen years.

- They tend to display shyness, blushing, and modesty.
- They become more interested in the opposite sex, but have mostly same sex friends, and date in groups.
- They move towards heterosexuality, with a temporary (in most cases) focus of same gender relationships.
- They have concerns regarding their own physical and sexual attractiveness to others.
- They move frequently from one relationship to another.
- They worry about being normal.
- They are concerned about other people's opinions of them.
- They spend considerable time on preparing their appearance and critiquing it in themselves, and others.

Educator and adolescent brain expert Sheryl Feinstein[1] states: "Adolescence is a time of startling growth and streamlining in the brain, enabling teenagers to think abstractly, speak expressively, and move gracefully."

Mentoring tip: As you look positively at your mentees, they start to change their views of themselves in a positive way.

---

1. Feinstein, *Secrets*, 167.

DAY 4: FEATURES OF ADOLESCENTS AGED BETWEEN THIRTEEN AND FIFTEEN (4)

Researchers highlight some common features of the majority of adolescents between the ages of thirteen and fifteen years when they discuss topics such as morals, values, and self-direction. Generally, youth

- test rules and limits;
- develop the capacity for abstract thought, and begin to understand ethical abstractions, such as honesty and justice;
- develop ideals and select role models;
- show more consistent evidence of having a conscience;
- experiment with sex and drugs (cigarettes, vaping, alcohol, marijuana);
- want their father's attention and influence;
- are influenced by the manner in which their parents resolve conflicts. Youth are likely to use the same approach to resolve conflicts later in life.

Mentors can reflect on these features. They might feel concerned about their mentee when the reality is that the young person is displaying normal teenage behavior. However, if concerning and negative patterns continue for an extended period of time, mentors should seek assistance from program staff, or others who work with adolescents.

Mentoring tip: Gently and sensitively coax your mentee to believe: "I can do it!"

MENTORING MOMENTS

How effectively can a mentor impact the life of a fifteen-year-old student over a nine-month school-based mentoring program which has a strong focus on youth being coached to appreciate that their lives have meaning and purpose? These comments written by mentees help answer that question.

> "[My mentor] has helped me through good times and bad and has helped me cope. She has also helped me with what my goal is in life and things I need to do to achieve becoming a teacher . . . [the program] has heaps of different aspects and it is brilliant . . . it is perfect the way it is."

"[My mentor] gave me a lot of confidence. He told me about my self-worth and my values. I was extremely lucky to get him as a mentor. I liked that I had someone to talk to whenever I needed to, through email and face to face. I realized throughout the journey my career goals and opportunities."

"My mentor has helped me analyse myself and the careers I'm interested in and helped me to find better time managing skills. I liked having someone to talk to about life in general, and having someone who can relate to certain things has been helpful and fun."

"She has really helped me with managing my time. She has also been a great help with finding information about my career and how to achieve it. I enjoyed the whole thing."

"She has helped me find what I'd like to do when I'm older and set a goal, as well as helping me find work experience at good places."

"Because I am 100 per cent sure about where I'm going in life and have gained many valuable skills that will help me achieve my goals. . . gained a friend."

"It was just good to be able to talk to someone about anything."

Mentoring tip: Look beneath the surface of appearances for whatever is real and lasting in yourself and others. Shed the masks, and remain true to yourself.

Week 19

DEALING WITH STRESS

Smiling stimulates our brain's reward mechanisms in a way that even chocolate, a well-regarded pleasure inducer, cannot match.

—Melissa Row

DAY 1: HOW TO RECOGNIZE STRESS

I am always on the lookout for possible signs of stress occurring *over an extended period of time* when I mentor adolescents.

Here are some signs to look out for which are documented in considerable research carried out over the years:

- intense, unnatural anxiety;
- body tension—tension headaches, and muscle tension anywhere in the body, but particularly in the neck, shoulders, back, and stomach;
- indigestion;
- sleep difficulties;
- nervousness;
- nausea, which could result in vomiting;
- poor self-image, low self-esteem, and feelings of incompetence;
- trembles and shakes; rushes around doing nothing; is clumsy, drops and breaks things; loses things;
- day-dreams; forgetful; concentrates poorly; believes that one has lost control and stability;
- becomes irritable in relationships; often blames others when things seem to go wrong; possibly also blames self excessively for relationship difficulties; aggressive behavior; appears self-absorbed;

- irregular breathing;
- a racing heartbeat;
- clenched jaw;
- panic attacks;
- unreasonable fear;
- feelings of oncoming doom and insanity—*I'm going crazy*!
- mood swings; extreme pessimism; a desire to run from it all;
- chronic tiredness;
- ongoing feelings of apathy;
- changes in appetite;
- tearfulness, or a desire to cry;
- loss of a sense of humor;
- difficulty with decision making.

Remember, if you are concerned about your mentee's health and well-being, seek guidance from someone more qualified and more experienced.

Mentoring tip: Always affirm your mentee's life, and encourage their potential to become the best they can be.

DAY 2: CAUSES AND EFFECTS OF STRESS

Mentors can discover the particular causes of a mentee's stress when they ask open-ended questions. Your mentee will share more with you as you build that trust bridge into your mentee's heart and mind. They learn how to appreciate that it is okay to be vulnerable in a non-judgmental, caring relationship.

Here are more possible causes of stress and anxiety:

- frustrations
- resentment
- anger
- hurt
- guilt
- aimlessness
- loneliness
- relationship problems
- losses
- crises
- failures
- setbacks

- grudges
- changes in personal situations (change of job; change of school; moves homes)
- denial—refuses to face up to an unpleasant reality
- lack of rest, exercise, or a healthy diet

Here are some possible results of feelings of stress being experienced by a mentee:

- anxiety
- a nervous breakdown
- obesity
- antisocial behavior
- fear
- smoking, or vaping
- depression
- suicide
- alcohol abuse
- drug abuse

You are the *significant other* the mentee needs in their life, as a supportive friend and mentor. Share a message like this with your mentee: "If you are able to change your attitude, make some positive choices, build new dreams, set realistic goals, and have the courage to face up to your situation, you can win through. I'll be alongside you to offer encouragement and support every step of the way."

Mentoring tip: Great mentors build character in their mentees as effective and authentic role models.

DAY 3: CHANNEL POSITIVE STRESS

Mentors help their mentees to understand the importance of positive stress in their daily lives as a way to motivate them to improve their performance. This understanding grows as you encourage and praise them, and work positively together towards the achievement of specific tasks, or goals.

Here are some helpful strategies I have followed with mentees.

- Promote and cultivate good daily habits.
- Be a role model who creates positive vibes that your mentee catches.
- Keep in touch with the evolving adolescent brain research.
- Dispense compassion with wisdom.

Never underestimate your power to build a positive and meaningful relationship with a young person.

Mental health expert Dr. John Arden[1] states: "study after study has shown that positive relationships are good for your health, particularly your immune system." He goes on to say: "Secure relationships form the basis for good mental and physical health."

Mentoring tip: Catch your mentee doing good. Send a text or a card; make a congratulatory certificate; write an email or note of praise, and you seed the mentor's spirit.

DAY 4: TEN RULES FOR A STRESS-LESS LIFE

In today's fast-paced world, there is increasing adolescent research which states that more young people appear to have greater levels of anxiety and stress than ever before. Quite some time ago I came across these ten rules for a stress-less life written by stress management expert David Lewis[2] which apply equally to adult mentors and adolescents.

Mentors can weave some of these suggestions into discussions with their mentees.

1. Never say never.
2. Act on facts, not assumptions.
3. Never generalize.
4. Accept your feelings.
5. Accept responsibility for yourself.
6. Abandon false hopes.
7. Step back from your problems.
8. Simplify your lifestyle.
9. Spend time with nature.
10. Make and take decisions with courage.

Mentoring tip: Mentors who genuinely encourage their mentees are never forgotten.

1. Arden, *Rewiring*.
2. Lewis, *One-minute Stress*.

MENTORING MOMENTS

Bella had struggled in her role at the school where I was the principal. Eventually we sat down, had an honest chat, and developed new strategies which I hoped would unlock Bella's potential.

This is part of Bella's story, which highlights the role of a mentor as an empathetic cheerleader:

> You know Robin, I never had anyone in my life that stood up for me and would take the time to mentor me. Your presence in my life was just what I needed at the time. I prayed hard for you to come along. For me, you were like the father I never had. You gave me the correct dose of unconditional love and discipline—sometimes not an easy task to do because I was so cheeky. There are not many people that are not afraid to stand up to me, and I really appreciated that you would not back down. You have a very special place in my heart . . . I just want to take time to thank you for taking time to see *me*—not my behavior—but my soul. I thank you for seeing potential in me when nobody else could. You really helped clear the filters that I used to filter through and this gave me the courage to go out and find ways to heal my soul on an even deeper level. I know that you risked a lot of yourself to stand up for me and took a lot of criticism. . . . But I really appreciate you trying to show the other side of who you experienced when we had one-on-one chats. Thank you for listening.

Mentoring tip: Always try to be well-organized, efficient, and able to weigh up options before you make a decision that will impact the life of a mentee with whom you connect and interact.

Week 20

CHALLENGING ISSUES

I am not a teacher, but an awakener.
—Robert Frost

DAY 1: DEAL WITH INAPPROPRIATE BEHAVIOR

A mentor might observe some concerning behavior over *an extended period of time*. This is dependent on a mentee's personal circumstances. Do your best to remain the non-judgmental cheerleader. Remain aware that some of this behavior *could* be linked to a poor self-image and low self-esteem.

Some possible signs of *inappropriate risk-taking*—usually, but not always involving life-threatening risks—might include:

- a fear of letting others down through not performing or not living up to their expectations;
- truancy;
- inappropriate sexual behavior;
- rebellious behavior;
- reckless driving;
- substance abuse.

Another area of possible concern is *inappropriate or insufficient sleep*. This may be caused by anxiety, or a variety of other factors, and can result in a lack of energy, listlessness, and a lack of motivation.

Never forget that you are neither a savior nor a rescuer, and you cannot fix families. Seek guidance and support from program staff, or people more experienced than you, as you develop a plan to encourage your mentee to reach their potential.

Mentoring tip: Remain aware that your mentee is a normal teenager when you observe problem behaviors, relationship instability, and feelings of inadequacy. Be a safety net to that young person.

DAY 2: LEARN TO MANAGE ANGER

Mentors coach their mentees how to manage anger, as most adolescents experience regular mood swings while the brain develops.

Here are a few proven strategies I have used when I mentor youth. The strategies follow many years of studying evidence-based research.

- Acknowledge and accept your mentee's feelings.
- Help your mentee verbalize their anger.
- Try to discover the root cause of your mentee's anger. Listen with an empathetic attitude. Ask open-ended questions, and do not pry.
- Understand how your mentee's culture deals with different kinds of conflict.
- Discuss the choices open to each one of us when we feel angry.
- Help your mentee to appreciate that, while it is normal to feel anger, it is not okay to hurt others, or hurt themselves, or hurt things.

Psychotherapist and author Gael Lindenfield[1] wrote: "Even children who are physically strong enough to defend themselves against an angry parent cannot be expected to have the emotional strength or same degree of behavioral skill with which to cope with this difficult emotion."

Your mentee grows to appreciate the importance of talking to someone—a peer and, preferably, a wise and trustworthy adult—about their anger as the connection in your mentoring relationship grows stronger.

Mentoring tip: Effective mentors confront their mentees honestly and directly because they care.

DAY 3: IDENTIFY MENTEES WITH A POOR SELF-IMAGE

Adolescent mentees with a poor self-image and low self-esteem find it harder to set goals, persevere, and reach their potential. Here are some signs to look out for, collated from evidence-based research in recent years.

---

1. Lindenfield, *Success*.

- Mentees seem preoccupied with self. They tend to seek distractions continually, may be workaholics, and appear more concerned with what they do, than who they become. They may see success and material possessions as a way to establish their identity and self-worth, even though they do not deal with "feelings" as they focus in these areas. For example, these mentees may feel that they have failed at school academically, or in games. They fear failure which can lead to an incomplete, or distorted self-image.
- Certain thoughts accompany their view of themselves as inferior and insignificant:
  - I am different from others.
  - I don't like myself.
  - I am useless.
  - Will I do well at school?
  - Nobody likes me.
  - I don't like being teased.
  - I wish I could change who I am.
- Although these preceding thoughts may also be found among mentees with higher self-esteem, for those with low self-esteem and a poor self-image such thoughts destroy their belief that they can achieve their ideal self-image.
  - I cannot meet my own goals.
  - My dreams and aspirations are meaningless.
  - I am only fooling myself.
  - It's too tough . . . I can't do it.
  - I am a loser.

A trusted mentor can help the young person make sense of possible confusion, and support them as they move forward at their chosen pace.

Mentoring tip: Teach mentees about their strengths. Name these specific strengths, as this builds resilience.

DAY 4: SUPPORT AND ENCOURAGE MENTEES

Here are a few thoughts to encourage mentors to work through challenging issues with their mentees.

- If your mentee has had privileges at home withdrawn, help them to understand the conflict resolution process. Discuss why the privileges have been withdrawn. Empathize and discuss ways your mentee can earn back the trust and privileges.

- Where appropriate, share difficulties you experienced as a teenager, how you overcame them, and any lessons you learned from them.

- Be sensitive and aware of any relevant school, home, or work difficulties your mentee experiences. You are there to *guide* your mentee, not to fix problems, or people.

- Understand that your mentoring relationship may experience some rocky times. This is natural when you mentor youth. Hang in there!

- Be prepared to seek advice, support, or assistance should you need it. If the issue relates to your mentee, it is appropriate to gain your mentee's permission to approach others on their behalf. Alternatively, you can offer to take your mentee to see someone who can help them.

- Describe the conflict resolution process in simple terms to your mentee. If you have resolved a conflict successfully, and used a particular method, share the experience. This is an effective way to begin a discussion on conflict resolution.

Mentoring tip: Always be sincerely and emotionally available to consistently draw alongside your mentee as a non-judgmental cheerleader.

MENTORING MOMENTS

A partnership between parents or caregivers and the mentors is a wonderful experience for any mentor. Some parents feel that they are poor role models to their children if mentors are required. They can be reassured, through quoting research, that youth require the support and encouragement of at least three significant adults during their adolescent years, as well as the love and support of their parents.

Parents commented on the impact of a nine-month school-based mentoring program on their fifteen-year-old children.

"[My son] has benefited enormously. He has a more positive attitude to his schooling career and is generally more focused. He has chosen appropriate decisions when interacting with his peers. I think it's a very valuable program and instils confidence, self-pride, and power to achieve. *Excellent!*"

"Has helped [my daughter] become work oriented, self-confident, self-motivated. The program has also given my daughter an independent view of the workplace."

"Good, wise influence. The caring influence being added to [my son's] growing up was priceless. Thanks for your efforts."

"My daughter seems very confident and can control situations in her life a lot better."

"[My son] was having some problems dealing with boys that were taunting or stirring him up. [His mentor] was able to provide an adult male perspective and help him through it. Many other things too. [My son] enjoyed the opportunity to discuss things confidentially with an adult male he trusted—would have liked it to go longer."

Mentoring tip: Make your life an example worth imitating to youth, and then sensitively invest some time and energy into their lives.

Week 21

MENTORING REFLECTIONS

Children will not remember you for the material things you provided, but for the feelings that you cherished within them.

—Richard L. Evans

DAY 1: CREATE ORDER OUT OF CHAOS

Our mentees experience some of the most confusing years of their lives as their brains develop.

Mentoring expert Edwin Bobrow[1] offers many positive mentoring strategies. Here are a few of his thoughts which I have paraphrased to assist mentors in their conversations with their mentees.

- It is important not to lose one's head, but to believe deep down that there is a way forward, a path into the future that can be chartered with the help of a mentor.
- Try and create positive thoughts and strategies through embracing positive thinking and a positive attitude.
- Keep exploring your mentee's dreams and visions about what they would like to achieve in the years ahead. This is where realistic goal setting is an important step in the long-term journey.
- Be the non-judgmental sounding board for your mentee, the person they can trust when they wish to share feelings and desires.
- Encourage your mentee to be patient with themselves, and "never" to fear failure as they strive to find the best way forward with your support.

---

1. Bobrow, *A mentor's guide*.

Mentoring tip: Effective mentors commit for the long-haul—half-hearted efforts are unacceptable.

DAY 2: MENTOR TRAINING FEEDBACK

I trained volunteer adult mentors to mentor youth for between nine and twelve months. I asked these mentors to write down one sentence to describe what they would have liked someone to say to them when they were adolescents. They shared their sentence with the group. This activity provided many ideas these mentors could take into their mentoring relationships.

> "You are a wonderful person as you are, and have so much to offer others right now."
>
> "I am proud of you in the way that you get things done when you say you are going to do them."
>
> "You have a lot to offer in the world and you *will* find your niche."
>
> "You are a person who is caring, supportive and really listens and understands."
>
> "You are a bubbly, caring, intelligent, genuine, attractive, and together person."
>
> "I am glad you are in my life. You make a difference in my life."
>
> "You have a great sense of humor—it is good to be able to laugh at life."

Remember how important it is to genuinely affirm mentees during the mentoring journey. What would you say to your mentee today?

Mentoring tip: Help your mentee gain some understanding of the real world of work by sharing your experiences.

DAY 3: SURGING SELF-WORTH

I remember a chat with a volunteer adult mentor. She expressed concern that she was making little headway in her relationship with her mentee in a school-based mentoring program.

I pointed out that her mentee was the first student to arrive each week for the mentoring meeting with his mentor. My assumption was that he valued and looked forward to their time together.

A surge of self-worth was occurring in this young man's life because his mentor, who had become a significant and wise adult in his life, consistently turned up for their meetings, and clearly enjoyed their time together. And, as they dialogued, the mentee experienced a self-discovery and a self-empowering journey. He worked out who he was, what his real interests were, and what direction he would pursue during his final years of school.

At the final celebratory event of the mentoring program, this young man stood up and publicly thanked his mentor for walking alongside him during the year. He had clear ideas about the careers he was interested in, and the subjects he needed to study. His self-confidence visibly increased as he shared with everyone present. His mentor smiled and remained humble, as I reminded her of our conversation a few months earlier.

Mentoring tip: Respect your mentee's privacy. As you connect, the "trust" door will swing open most of the time.

DAY 4: "10 TICKETS" TO MENTORING

Mentoring expert Thomas W. Dortch Jr.[2], shared his "10 Tickets" to mentoring, collated after looking at a Gallup poll of male mentors, aged between twenty and sixty, with an average age of forty-eight, most of whom had some form of tertiary education.

The "10 Tickets" is a helpful checklist for mentors of adolescents, as it promotes the spirit of mentoring.

1. Take ownership of the fact that mentoring is about creating a meaningful relationship with a mentee.
2. Always act as a role model for your mentee.
3. Talk openly with your mentee about what is right and wrong.
4. Model wholesome values to your mentee.
5. Enjoy the mentoring journey because you believe that you have something positive to offer your mentee.
6. Work hard to develop a trusting relationship with your mentee.
7. Make sure your mentee hears that you genuinely care about them.
8. Guide your mentee so he or she understands the most appropriate behavior for certain situations.

---

2. Dortch Jr., *The Miracles*, 64.

9. Assist your mentee with the goal getting journey.
10. Be available to listen to whatever your mentee wants to share with you.

Mentoring tip: Teach your mentee how to admit mistakes, and learn from them. That is how resiliency is developed.

MENTORING MOMENTS

Dave Lewis taught me English and History and was my hockey coach for two years. In my sixth form year—my final year of school—he was my tutor.

Dave was also a hockey player. We played for the same hockey club—different teams—on a Saturday afternoon. We enjoyed numerous chats about life when our paths crossed.

Dave was a significant adult during an important season in my life, as my brain developed, and I tried to make sense of a great deal of confusion. What was my meaning and purpose in life?

Dave had a wonderful sense of humor, was humble, and modeled the importance of social justice. He never followed the crowd, and was prepared to stand up and be counted when he believed strongly about a particular issue. He coached me how to be vulnerable, to stand tall in the face of adversity, and to step out of my comfort zone.

Later in my career, when Dave heard I was looking for a History teaching position, he contacted me and, through his advocacy, I was offered the job being advertised at the time.

When Dave moved into a senior management position, he passed the batons of the Head of History faculty, and teacher in charge of hockey over to me. He believed in me, supported and encouraged me, and was a mentor and friend in different seasons of my life. He modeled the spirit of mentoring.

Mentoring tip: Model a clearly defined set of values when you wish to positively connect, and build meaningful relationships with your mentee.

Week 22

FATIGUE

> We are not machines. We are people with our own finger-prints of personality and potential.
>
> —William Pollard

DAY 1: UNDERSTAND FATIGUE (1)

Mentors help their mentees to understand that at times they will feel fatigued. This is natural in everyone's life. Share ways to identify and deal with these times.

- Research states that everyone experiences about two hours of fatigue every day. The common times are after lunch, or immediately after school, or work.

- According to one school of thought, we will feel fatigued for twenty minutes out of every ninety minutes. Fatigue passes and then we are alert again. (No one seems to know why!) So, for example, if a mentee studies for forty to forty-five minutes cycles, with a five to ten minutes break after each cycle, they will work more consistently at the peak performance level.

- Level of exercise can be a way to cope with fatigue, and can also increase, or reduce stress. Here are some exercise tips.
    - If mentees are not sporty or do not like going to a gym, a fast walk for thirty minutes every second day will probably keep them in shape. I have personally witnessed a number of young lives transformed when these young people undertook a simple, *consistent* exercise program of their choice.

- Sports like swimming and cycling are excellent sports to keep healthy.
- Mentees can keep a log-book of their exercise efforts—use the back of a diary. They can set mini-goals for themselves. For example, cover a certain distance within a specific time period.

Mentoring tip: Great mentoring helps to shape and influence your mentees to fulfill their potential.

DAY 2: UNDERSTAND FATIGUE (2)

The mentoring relationship allows time to discuss the importance of a healthy and balanced lifestyle for the developing brain. Mentors help their mentees understand the importance of a healthy diet. This is a major topic that can be discussed fairly regularly. However, discuss a topic like this sensitively, as much will depend on the mentee's home circumstances.

A poor diet is likely to contribute to longer periods of fatigue.

- Research shows that while the body must have fat to live on, if we consume too much fat during a meal—including fried food, or "junk" food—our mental and physical efforts slow down for nearly two hours afterwards. Digestion demands between 40 percent and 60 percent of our available physical and mental energy. The result is weariness and a lack of motivation.
- A heavy sugar-loading in drinks—soft drinks, tea, or coffee—contributes to fatigue. Sugar causes the blood-sugar level to increase, triggering the insulin response to reduce the blood-sugar level quickly. This can leave you feeling exhausted.
- Beware of drinking too much coffee. Caffeine overstimulates the adrenal glands, which initially makes you feel more switched on and alert, but can lead to fatigue in the longer term.

Also encourage your mentee to have a healthy breakfast every day, as this enhances learning outcomes, and positive brain activity.

Mentoring tip: Remind your mentee that anyone can be a success if they set realistic, achievable goals, and work "consistently" to achieve them.

DAY 3: STRATEGIES TO DEAL WITH STRESS AND FATIGUE (1)

Mentors can encourage their mentees to deal with stress and fatigue in positive ways. These could become targets for goal setting as a means to assist mentees to reach their potential.

Here are some positive strategies to discuss with your mentees at an appropriate time.

- Face up to any problems or issues. Seek help. Determine to overcome these problems and take charge of your life. You make *choices*. You are *accountable and responsible* for your actions.
- Take one day at a time, and one step at a time.
- Improve your management of time and daily planning where necessary.
- Carry out daily relaxation exercises. Mentors can share some well-known breathing and reflective exercises with mentees.
- Do not quit! Switch gears and move from a high-level concentration project to something less demanding.
- Highlight the importance of nine hours of sleep *every* night. Brain research states that the pruning of the brain takes place when the adolescent sleeps. Sleep is the glue that allows us to recollect our experiences, and to remember everything we have learnt during the day.

Mentoring tip: Cultivate the art of solving daily problems creatively, while being able to remain somewhat detached about them, and observe your mentee soar.

DAY 4: STRATEGIES TO DEAL WITH STRESS AND FATIGUE (2)

An important role mentors can play in the lives of their mentees is to help these young people develop strategies to create the right balance in their lives.

Here are some helpful strategies to share with mentees.

- Write out reasons for fears, anxieties or worries, which can lead to a solution. Take the worst possible outcome. Consider how you can minimize it when you use every means in your power. You may surprise yourself when you begin to focus on positive solutions.

- Drink two to three glasses of water and repeat the process fifteen minutes later. This activates the lymphatic system and flushes out toxins, including lactic acid, the main physical cause of fatigue.
- Sit up straight. Breathe in deeply to a count of two. Exhale slowly to a count of between four and ten.
- Sit up, or stand up, to increase the supply of oxygen in the blood, which then carries the oxygen to your brain, and causes you to feel more alert. It is like turning on a light switch.
- Take a few minutes to clear the mind completely. You might do something physical, like take a short walk. Switch from logical thinking to creative thinking. For example, when you study cloud formations, or a picture, or a poster, you let the imagination flow.
- Refocus on your goals, which is why you keep them in a handy place. Check that you have realistic and measurable action steps set for each day, and each week.

Mentoring tip: Courageous mentors are real, present, vulnerable, and responsive with their mentees.

MENTORING MOMENTS

I have loved training peer mentors and sowing the seeds of mentoring. Each time I read the evaluations after the training, I am reminded that every person is unique, and these seventeen-year-old students have great insights.

These comments were made at the end of a one-day training program in response to a question: what were the most important lessons you learnt today?

> "Try hard to get involved in the activities; we should take care of each other; be positive about yourself and your situations; smile!"

> "Working in groups is fun; there are some people who may appreciate my help; I am an ok person; communication is important."

> "People who I think did not like me, do admire my qualities; if you are honest to yourself, people will respect you; others are feeling and going through exactly what I am going through."

"There are lots of groups around to support us; a good leader is motivational; a good friend must have a good sense of humor; most people have similar anxieties when approaching people in a new school."

"Aware of other people's opinions; deeper understanding about myself; feeling better, ready to help new students; practice working in a team."

"Gossiping is very dangerous and the story can get "very" twisted; it is important for young people to have an older friend to look to for guidance and support; there are many virtues needed to be a good leader; at a new school, students need to feel comfortable."

Mentoring tip: Strive to be an exemplary role model and wise advocate, a positive, non-judgmental influence in the lives of youth.

Week 23

ACHIEVE GOALS

A child's life is like a piece of paper on which every person leaves a mark.

—CHINESE PROVERB

DAY 1: KEY RESULTS OF A REALISTIC GOAL SETTING PROCESS

These are some key results of a goal-setting process. Share them with your mentee at appropriate times during the mentoring journey.

- A goal-setting process gives us a sense of purpose and security, and a focus as we learn more about who we are.
- It helps us achieve more with our lives, and reminds us that we choose to have control over our lives and make things happen. With it we can build our lives on firm foundations.
- It helps us to organize our resources effectively.
- Goal setting helps eliminate negative attitudes that can cause unhappiness and self-doubt.
- It improves our management of time and results in a happier and more balanced quality of life.
- Effective goal setting reduces stress and anxiety.
- It improves concentration, and it teaches us how to deal with setbacks so that we see them as opportunities for learning. We learn how to see failure as a positive opportunity to identify which skills and areas of performance we can improve.

- Goal setting improves performance and boosts self-esteem, self-confidence, and self-belief.
- It teaches us how to have a long-term vision and short-term action plans.
- Goal setting teaches us how to move out of our comfort zone and take calculated, non-life-threatening risks.

Mentoring tip: Help your mentee hold on to bold dreams as you work together to achieve small, realistic, and measurable action steps.

DAY 2: USE A DIARY

One observation in recent years, as the digital age takes hold of our lives, is a general deterioration in the planning, organization, and management of time skills of many adolescents.

Adolescent brain research stresses the importance of coaching adolescents how to use a paper diary and write down their schedules, rather than use an electronic diary. Youth are training their brain, and this activity helps them manage their time and organize tasks.

Mentees develop greater self-discipline, and have an easy way to monitor the progress of action plans which can be discussed with their mentors. This teaches them the meaning of accountability and, as they complete tasks by the set deadlines, they enhance the opportunities to reach their potential.

Mentoring tip: Reinforce the importance for your mentee to stay in school, develop good work habits, and make the right choices to help them reach their potential.

DAY 3: GUIDE MENTEES THROUGH THE GOAL GETTING PROCESS

Mentors coach their mentees to appreciate that the goal getting process includes frustrations, failures and doing things they "have" to do, even when they do not wish to do so—such as certain school academic subjects—and that they can positively respond to these challenges.

The aim is for mentees to become goal getters who seek to attain the outcomes they want. That is, they clarify the outcome, then focus their efforts with a specific plan that mentors help them develop. In this way, mentees take ownership of the choices they make.

Mentees become informed learners, and develop important life skills as they learn how to actively participate in the process, and how to persist when the going is tough.

Mentees will probably become more excited, enthusiastic, self-confident, and motivated after they define their goals. They start to feel in control of their lives, and more able to cope with the storms along the way.

In contrast, where mentees do not have goals, researchers state that they are more prone to negative emotions like frustration, anger, boredom, loneliness, fear, and depression, which can lead to antisocial behavior.

Mentoring tip: Effective mentors build their mentees up, encourage them, correct them, stretch them, and sustain them every step of the mentoring journey.

DAY 4: KEY GOAL SETTING TIPS FOR MENTORS

Mentors play a significant role as they guide and coach their mentees how to set and achieve their goals.

Here are a few tips that are often forgotten when we guide youth how to set and achieve goals, all of which I follow when I mentor young people.

- Make sure that your mentee has a clear and realistic plan of action in place to achieve their "personal" goal, or goals.
- Encourage your mentee to have a clear picture, like an imaginary personal photograph, of them achieving their goal. Always encourage them to write each goal as a positive visualization statement which they can refer to every day.
- Make sure that each goal is aligned to your mentee's values, their mission, and purpose in life.
- Encourage your mentees to rid themselves of the negative factors and, wherever possible, the negative people in their lives.
- Guide your mentees how to use their failures as learning experiences from which to plan for future successes to reach their potential.

Mentoring tip: Your mentees need your assistance as they consider options and opportunities—you are an awesome resource.

MENTORING MOMENTS

Charles was homesick for a couple of months when he entered the boarding house. He was a talented sportsman who had to work hard at his academic studies to fulfill his potential. There were a couple of conversations between his mother and me, when she wondered if the correct decision had been made to send Charles to boarding school. I encouraged her to give Charles more time to settle.

Charles and I spent time chatting about his friendships, his feelings, considered his long-term sports goals, and shared other life experiences. There were some challenging moments. At the end of the year his mother wrote me this note:

> I would like to take this opportunity of thanking you for all you have done for Charles while he has been at [the school]. You have understood him and given him the right kind of encouragement and motivation. . . . I appreciate the care and counselling you gave him during that time. He has changed a lot this year, and I find many positive qualities that I know you have helped to nurture. I just hope that Charles will be sufficiently self-motivated to obtain the goals that he is so capable of reaching. Only time will tell. You have certainly set him on the right road.

Charles achieved competent academic grades, a university degree, entered the world of commerce, and was selected for his state in two sports.

Mentoring tip: Your character, sense of commitment, and expression of unconditional love will determine the effectiveness of your connection with youth.

Week 24

LISTEN! LISTEN!

> We must view young people not as empty bottles to be filled, but as candles to be lit.
>
> —Robert Shaffer

DAY 1: THE GIFT OF LISTENING

Authentic mentors spend time with their mentees, and show a sincere interest in youth. They explore interests and dreams, chat about goal setting, look for opportunities to affirm their mentees as they journey together, and always celebrate the small and large victories.

Listening is a key quality required for this mentoring relationship to develop meaningfully. Communication expert Anne Long[1] wrote:

> Just listening can be a far greater gift than the listener realizes, whatever the age of the person being listened to. Listening to another person is a way of giving him or her worth, of valuing them. It is not second best to speaking. It is a gift in its own right and something we can all do. When I listen to someone carefully, I give space to allow them to express themselves. This can be a great gift in today's busy life when everyone is in a hurry.

As mentors, be inspired by the words of African poet, Antoine-Roger Bolamba: "What we need is a happiness bridge where two hearts that are strangers can make an exchange of their gifts."

Mentoring tip: Allow your mentee to observe you doing something inspiring, and share your strengths.

---

1. Long, *Listening*.

DAY 2: CONFLICT RESOLUTION: THREE KEY AREAS IN THE PROCESS

Mentors can coach and teach adolescent mentees how to positively react to conflict situations when they understand these three key areas:

Firstly, have an *awareness* of

- beliefs and responses that perpetuate human behavior and know how they usually respond to conflict—go on the defensive, deny the conflict, or feel defeated by the conflict.

Secondly, show a *willingness* to

- experiment with new approaches;
- revisit their belief structures;
- look at conflict in a new light.

Thirdly, learn the *key skills* of how to

- convey an effective message in a non-threatening way;
- honestly state their feelings;
- state their needs;
- listen effectively.

Mentoring tip: A sustained human relationship is the essence of mentoring—listen, nurture, support, advise, and care for your mentee.

DAY 3: GOOD FOCUS

A meaningful mentoring relationship between a mentor and a mentee requires mentors to have a positive and encouraging attitude to put your mentees at ease. Be interested. Create a positive atmosphere through non-verbal behavior when you communicate.

- Lean forward slightly to show interest.
- Establish good eye contact.
- Gaze steadily with friendliness and warmth.
- Use tone of voice to demonstrate understanding.
- Use non-verbal acknowledgments—nod, or match facial expressions to those of your mentee.

Increase the self-awareness of your mentees. Share experiences, encourage the development of new skills, such as art, drama, or music, and make them aware of different emotions.

Healthy discussions help mentees to discover what is close to their heart and what interests them. On occasions, play devil's advocate. I tell mentees when I play devil's advocate, because I want them to be challenged, to think, and not feel threatened.

I also ban the phrase, "I don't know." My response to that statement is: "That's a forbidden phrase in my presence. You have a good brain. Use it." I say this in a gentle, affirming, and non-threatening way. As I connect with my mentee, and share that expression, it creates smiles.

Mentoring tip: Great mentors guide their mentees to understand and live out the meaning of perseverance.

DAY 4: A FEW BASIC RULES

A challenge for twenty-first century educators is to train all students to become peer mentors at some point during their high school years. Once they have served as peer mentors for a year, they develop a growth mindset that will assist their future development, and give them a greater sense of meaning and purpose.

A group of seventeen-year-old students completed a one-day peer mentor training program. Reflect on the similarities and differences in their feedback, as well as some wonderful insights. We are unique! These students were asked to highlight the most important "things" they gained from the day.

> "Speak out! There's nothing to lose; don't be afraid to help people."
>
> "Understand and remember how others feel; traits to be a better person."
>
> "Smile and enjoy life; group or community benefit goes first; care about others more."
>
> "Gossiping distorts facts; your body language encourages and discourages someone else; it's important to participate."
>
> "Have good body language expressing your listening; don't gossip, it hurts; don't just pay attention to your friends, but everyone."

"To have the chance to know someone we haven't known before; to speak our opinions openly; teamwork is important; I feel respectful."

"To recognize how I can help new students; the ability to see constructively what my weaknesses are; learnt more about my classmates."

"Everyone has good qualities; how to communicate effectively with others; small actions of kindness can mean a lot to the recipient."

Mentoring tip: Researchers note that longer mentoring relationships lead to greater levels of self-worth, better social skills, and improved academic results.

MENTORING MOMENTS

Our mentees are unique individuals. This is evident when one reads some of the mentors' comments at the conclusion of a nine-month school-based mentoring program. Students were fifteen-years-of-age from a variety of socio-economic backgrounds.

"I noticed a general change in attitude over the time. [My mentee] became more positive overall. Coordinator and support/training was fantastic."

"Able to introduce [her] to someone whose support enabled her to identify her strengths and weaknesses and career preferences. The fact that she will return to the school next year is a plus, as she had earlier planned to move schools."

"His attitude has changed. He is happier with himself and has made new friends."

"I think [he] has become more positive, more engaged at school. I really enjoyed him starting to open up to me. He doesn't talk much to his family, so it was very rewarding."

"Introduced some hard realities of leaving school at the end of this year or in two years' time; took practical step in taking [him] to work place; relaxed approach, taking day to day issues as they come; reflected on links to family, both work and relationships."

Mentoring tip: Your role is to genuinely inspire, motivate, and encourage young people to attain realistic, measurable, and achievable performance goals which they have chosen.

Week 25

GENERAL ISSUES

> Whatever you can do, or dream you can... begin it. Boldness has genius, power and magic in it.
>
> —Johann Wolfgang Von Goethe

DAY 1: CROSS-CULTURAL MENTORING

Culture, in its broadest sense, is the underlying fabric that holds together a person's world. In other words, it is just about everything that binds a person to a particular group, and time. It includes our language, values, beliefs, customs, rituals, oral and written history, art, music, dance, food, and much more.

The primary job of a mentor of adolescents is to honor the inherent worth that each young person brings into the world and to respect their special cultural background. Researcher Linda Jucovy[1] described how exercising this respect means that mentors will

- honestly examine their own mind for prejudices and stereotypes (given that almost all of us have learned some);
- think about where their biases come from, and try to see them as learned misinformation;
- make a personal commitment to be a culturally sensitive mentor;
- see their mentee, first and foremost, as a unique and valuable person;
- approach cultural differences as an opportunity for learning.

In my cross-cultural mentoring experiences, I have found mentees love to talk and teach me about their culture. We discuss cultural attitudes

---

1. Jucovy, *Same-race*.

to family, money, marriage, teachers or authority figures, faith, conflict, and how I would be expected to behave if I visited my mentee's home. These are enriching conversations.

Mentoring tip: Familiarize yourself with the music, movies, TV programs, social media, and other forms of entertainment with which your mentee might identify. These are great talking points—empathy in action!

DAY 2: LEARN ABOUT THE POSITIVES OF CONFLICT

Encourage your mentees to look at conflict as having a *positive* value. When handled constructively, conflict helps us to

- learn new and better ways to respond to problems;
- build better and more durable relationships;
- learn more about ourselves and others.

Above all, you can help your mentees to identify what style of behavior they follow when they face conflicts. If their style tends to perpetuate the conflict, you can share different methods of conflict resolution to break a negative conflict cycle. (The different conflict styles are covered in Mentoring Minute messages—Week 13)

New Zealand parenting expert Ian Grant[2] offers three behavior skills which we can discuss with our mentees. These three skills assist their thinking when they are caught up in a conflict situation.

1. Walk away until you have calmed down.
2. Think about whether it matters or not.
3. Remind yourself that it is okay if things don't always go your way— you can handle it.

Mentoring tip: Continually remind your mentee to turn obstacles into positive, and possibly life-changing opportunities.

DAY 3: TIPS TO NURTURE RESILIENT MENTEES

A key role of an effective volunteer adult mentor is to develop resilient mentees. How can you do this?

---

2. Grant, *Fathers.*

Here are a few ideas and strategies that I have used effectively for many years. The key point is that they are non-threatening, motivating and even, in some instances, inspiring.

- Focus on the development of a caring, trusting relationship with your mentees, and not on saving them.
- Have fun together.
- Have positive, high, realistic expectations for your mentees.
- Never quit on your mentees.
- Meet your mentees' emotional safety needs by being available to talk. Sustain kindness, for example, with a touch on the shoulder, a smile, or a genuine greeting.
- Get to know your mentees' strengths, dreams, and gifts. Help them to develop the skills and resources to unlock these. You convey the message: *You matter.*
- Be reliable and accessible, and turn up for the agreed meetings with your mentees.
- Encourage your mentees to create positive peer groups—that is, small groups to help build a positive community.
- Respect, take an interest in, actively listen to, and validate the feelings of a struggling mentee in a non-judgmental manner.
- Encourage your mentees to involve themselves in extracurricular activities, such as art, music, cultural activities, community projects, or service activities in or out of school.

Mentoring tip: Encourage, affirm, and cheer your mentee on to greater heights.

DAY 4: INCONSISTENT BEHAVIOR PATTERNS

A mentor has the challenging role to nurture a mentee during an emotional, physical, and socially difficult stage of their lives.

You could observe patterns of behavior over an *extended period* of time that *could* be warning bells linked to poor self-image, and low self-esteem.

Here are three areas to consider.

1. *Changes in communication styles and attitudes* (which often starts at home and then becomes evident in school):

    - more aggressive language;
    - use of put downs;
    - pessimism;
    - compulsive lying;
    - disruptive behavior;
    - bullying;
    - avoidance of challenge, and fear of failure and mistakes;
    - attention seeking (displaying a dependence on others);
    - withdrawal from communication.

2. *Changes in emotion.* Here you look out for:

    - temper tantrums;
    - inappropriate crying;
    - hypersensitivity to criticism;
    - a tendency to be easily upset by mistakes;
    - apparently inexplicable mood swings;
    - defiant behavior;
    - intolerance of others;
    - unrelenting grief;
    - emotional withdrawal.

3. *Frequent illnesses, accidents, and obsessive behavior:*

    - a feeling of rejection by peers because of the mentee's physical appearance;
    - eating disorders—eating too much, or too little;
    - excessive diligence about schoolwork;
    - obsession with fitness—inappropriate aerobics, jogging, or gym workouts;

- an over-involvement in sports activities which might be a convenient distraction from an issue the young person is dealing with.

Mentoring tip: Great mentors include their mentees in their lives. "Always" be genuine.

MENTORING MOMENTS

Many students regarded the exceptionally talented classics teacher Mike Fisher as eccentric. He had some strange mannerisms, yet was a complete all-rounder—teacher, coach, musician, chorister, dramatist, and sportsman.

Mike was my cricket coach for three years. I was captain of the team for about fifteen months. We would spend hours discussing team selections and strategies. Mike was fiercely competitive, yet also scrupulously honest and fair. He had a wicked sense of humor, and often poked fun at himself.

The silent messages Mike put across to me were: "You matter and I respect your opinion." "I believe in you."

Mike was a stickler for doing the basics well, and taking a pride in one's appearance. He modeled this, and coached me how to develop these skills and share them with many teams I coached during my career. He also modeled good planning and management of time.

I treasured a card he sent me at the end of my final year at school, and after I had been selected for my state cricket team.

> Many congratulations on an excellent year in every way—cricket and otherwise . . . The very best of luck for the [inter-state] week, and for the future, and thank you for all you did for school cricket this year—it will not be forgotten, nor has it gone unnoticed.

Mike modeled the importance of being oneself at all times, as well as giving me insight into the meaning and application of the spirit of mentoring.

Mentoring tip: Guide, encourage, and teach youth that, "most" of the time, they are responsible for their choices, actions and consequences of those choices.

Week 26

RELATIONSHIPS

> The meaning of life is to find your gift; the purpose of life is to give it away.
>
> —Joy Golliver

DAY 1: LIFE SUCCESS AND A MENTOR'S SECRET

Well-known author, Ted Engstrom, stated: "Our greatest mentors are those who are also our models. . . .. The secret of mentoring in any field is to help a person get to where he or she is willing to go." Reflect on these wonderful words of encouragement to any mentors.

Pastor Bob Kraning commented: "the ultimate success of my life will not be judged by the number of those who admire me for my accomplishments, but by the number of those who attribute their wholeness to my love for them—by the number of those who have seen their true beauty and worth in my eyes."

There are no perfect mentors and there is no perfect way to mentor, as our mentees are unique individuals in a different head space. Mentees want a significant, non-judgmental cheerleader in their lives who, through their actions, conveys two important messages: "I am here for you!" and, "I believe in you!"

Mentoring tip: Courageous mentors express unconditional love and care that nurtures and inspires their mentees.

DAY 2: RELATE TO YOUR MENTEES

Relating to adolescent mentees is as easy as expressing a genuine interest in them. Spend time with them. Share with them. Listen to them. Continually work at the development of the skill of reflective listening—when an adolescent tells you about a problem, or issue, repeat what they share in your own words. You might say, for example: "As I understand it, you are saying..." or, "What I think you are saying is..."

You must have a sense of peace about yourself and who you are, so you can feel more comfortable about giving of yourself to others and being vulnerable in their presence.

There are many rewards when you encourage and support adolescent mentees. Here are some examples of what they receive, collated from many years of evidence-based research.

- Increased feelings of self-worth.
- A sense of belonging.
- A better perspective on themselves.
- A feeling of significance.
- A sense of hope about who they can become.

Mentoring tip: It is okay for your mentee to make mistakes that are not life-threatening. Reach out a hand, and encourage your mentee along the road ahead.

DAY 3: A MENTEE REFLECTS

I talk and share a lot about the mentor as a positive role model in the young person's life, as the latter's brain continues to develop. Youth research states that these young people need a consistent, caring, committed, and reliable significant other in their lives.

I remember reading the account of an adolescent mentee who described how she had to work hard not to allow her mentor to become too actively involved in her life. She felt that she had to show her mentor that she could move forward as an independent free spirit. Yet she always felt her mentor was a "secret weapon" in her life.

What she meant was that, when she faced a challenge, she would hear the stable, non-judgmental, and encouraging voice of her mentor in her head. It felt that, through the mentoring relationship, a part of the mentor lived within her, something she felt privileged to possess.

This young girl shared how one day she imagined herself calling her mentor to invite her for dinner, during which time she would share all she had done since the formal mentoring relationship had ended. She envisioned her mentor being as proud of her as she was of herself, because she had lived the life she and her mentor had imagined and dreamed of during the mentoring journey.

What a wonderful testament to the spirit of mentoring.

Mentoring tip: An effective mentor never accepts verbal abuse, or physical intimidation.

DAY 4: SHARE LIFE EXPERIENCES

One of the great ways for mentors to connect with their mentees is to share life experiences.

One day you want your mentee to grasp the importance of a mentoring relationship, and to pass the mentoring baton to the next generation.

So, share your experiences as an adolescent with your mentee. Talk about the people who took on mentoring roles in your life, what they said and shared with you, favorite quotes and, most especially, *why* and *how* they impacted your life in such a positive way. Chat, too, about other mentors you have had since your school days.

You want your mentee to feel that they know your mentors as you share your experiences. As this happens, you sow the seeds of the spirit of mentoring in a young life. You share exactly what your mentee expects of you—someone to have open and honest discussions about life, career opportunities, what may or may not be possible, and how to be open-minded and risk failure as they move out of their comfort zone.

Most important, as you experienced with your mentors, your mentee knows that you are a non-judgmental cheerleader, and a consistent presence for a while in their life.

Mentoring tip: Effective mentors reflect the deepest truths of their lives, and leave an imprint on their mentees' hearts.

MENTORING MOMENTS

One learns a great deal about team members when one has the privilege of spending time with them in the pre-tour training, and then during the overseas trip. Throughout these trips one also has the opportunity to sow the seeds of the spirit of mentoring, and model important life skills, and values.

Seventeen-year-old Guy was a student on one tour. This is what he wrote on his return home:

Whether we won or lost is important, because everyone likes winning, but not as important as the other things that occurred on the tour. Like the amount I learnt about hockey. My game has shown tremendous improvement which is largely thanks to you. ... Apart from the hockey, another aspect I enjoyed was the great friendship shown among the boys and the [teachers]. This showed everywhere and never faltered. Thank you very much for what you did for the tour whether it be the organization, the coaching, or the maintenance of team spirit.

Mentoring tip: Always appreciate that positive role models understand that the attitude of their heart is more important and more obvious than anything they say when communicating with youth.

Week 27

FEATURES OF ADOLESCENTS AGED BETWEEN SIXTEEN AND EIGHTEEN

The future belongs to those who believe in the beauty of their dreams.
—Eleanor Roosevelt

DAY 1: FEATURES OF ADOLESCENTS AGED BETWEEN SIXTEEN AND EIGHTEEN (1)

In the period between the ages of sixteen and eighteen adolescents move from interdependence to independence. As you take account of their reality, encourage your mentees to become *interdependent*, always staying connected to their family or extended family. Much will depend on the mentee's family situation, of course.

Generally, youth in this age group

- function independently more often;
- have a firmer, more cohesive sense of identity;
- examine their inner experiences;
- are able to think ideas through;
- spend less time in conflict with their parents or caregivers;
- are more able to delay gratification and to compromise;
- are more emotionally stable;
- are more concerned for others;
- are more self-reliant;

- still regard peer relationships as important and give them an appropriate place among other interests, though they may be less likely to conform to peer pressure;
- boys in particular experience deepened voices, added muscle, and reduced body fat, become less self-conscious and self-focused, and combine features of the self into an organized self-concept.

Mentoring tip: Your mentee's future is at stake. Never hesitate to seek advice, support, and encouragement from program staff, other mentors, or other adults who work with youth.

DAY 2: FEATURES OF ADOLESCENTS AGED BETWEEN SIXTEEN AND EIGHTEEN (2)

Most adolescents between the ages of sixteen and eighteen look into the future and seek meaning and purpose at a time when cognitive changes occur.

Generally, young people

- define their work habits more clearly;
- become more concerned for the future;
- give more importance to their role in life;
- begin to associate with social issues;
- become interested in philosophical, ethical, and religious issues and challenges;
- become more socially aware and responsible;
- have aspirations that may exceed their capabilities;
- understand relationships between cause and effect;
- are better at everyday planning and decision making;
- evaluate vocational options in terms of interests, abilities, and values.

Collated research states that a large proportion of teenagers begin to disassociate from their fathers by the age of seventeen, and expectation levels decline accordingly, especially among boys. This is one reason a mentor can play a significant role during this time of transition to independence and more independent thinking.

Mentoring tip: Encourage mentees to set goals that are consistent with their values, and share some of your goals as a positive role model.

DAY 3: FEATURES OF ADOLESCENTS AGED BETWEEN SIXTEEN AND EIGHTEEN (3)

It is helpful for a mentor to have some knowledge of the features around the sexuality of the *majority* of adolescents aged between the ages of sixteen and eighteen. Generally, young people

- experience feelings of love and passion;
- develop more serious relationships;
- have a firmer sense of their sexual identity;
- have a greater capacity for tender and sensual love;
- begin to have opposite sex friends and to date alone;
- often are more sexually active by the age of sixteen or seventeen (in some cases, maybe earlier);
- girls complete their growth spurt during this time.

Brain researcher and medical expert Dr. Francis Jensen[1] states: "Teenagers may look like adults, they may even think like adults in many ways, and their ability to learn is staggering, but knowing what teenagers are unable to do—what their cognitive, emotional and behavioral limitations are, is critical."

Mentoring tip: Great mentors are effective and authentic role models who build character in their mentees.

DAY 4: FEATURES OF ADOLESCENTS AGED BETWEEN SIXTEEN AND EIGHTEEN (4)

Mentoring an adolescent as they become a more independent spirit between sixteen and eighteen years of age is both a challenging and exciting time. You will find that the *majority* of young people display some of the following features:

- they have a greater capacity to set goals;
- they are more interested in moral reasoning;

1. Jensen, *The Teenage Brain*.

FEATURES OF ADOLESCENTS AGED BETWEEN SIXTEEN AND EIGHTEEN

- they acquire the capacity to use insight;
- they give greater emphasis to personal dignity and self-esteem;
- they place importance on social and cultural traditions;
- they explore vocational interests;
- they are more likely to search for meaning and purpose in life;
- they are likely to register greater stress than younger teenagers, because they experience many new and significant pressures. Some of the more common pressures would include:
  - the physical maturation stage concludes;
  - they have a keen interest in dating;
  - peer acceptance is important to them;
  - they begin to explore sexual opportunities;
  - uncertainties about a post-school education and career;
  - driving and related expenses receive a focus;
  - academic performance pressures impact their lives;
  - the impact of social media on their lives;
  - moral and ethical challenges become significant in many young people's lives.

Consult with experienced program staff or professionals who work with youth when a mentee appears quite different from those described in the general messages shared during the past four days. There might be specific mental health issues, or gender issues, or antisocial behavior concerns. Every young person is unique with special gifts and talents to make a positive difference in the world—*never* forget this.

Mentoring tip: Create new opportunities and learning experiences for your mentee when you spend time together. You enrich a young life.

MENTORING MOMENTS

Bella's story was shared earlier in the book (Week 19, Mentoring moments). Bella moved from her school role to forge a new career path. She obtained a university degree, and then launched a successful business which helps people who face a variety of challenges.

As Bella studied, she had to share her story with a tutor—Caroline. The tutor then had to contact the mentor or person who had had a significant influence in Bella's life.

We all value affirmation. This note from Caroline is special because it encouraged me to continue the development of mentoring skills, and eventually to set up a website to share resources with others. It also reminded me how important it is for a mentee to feel safe and secure in the presence of their mentor at all times. I remain humbled when I read Caroline's note all these years later.

This is an extract from the letter Caroline wrote to me after her interview with Bella.

> I hope this letter helps give you some clarity on the powerful and profound effect you have had on this most amazing woman [Bella]. I have a feeling that you are proud and/or privileged to have been involved with such a well-adjusted, intelligent and self-aware woman.
>
> Robin, I'd like to request that you continue to nurture this amazing part of your personality—the ability to recognize and nurture potential, your genuine care, and your support. With such talents you could have a greatly profound influence on the world around you.
>
> It was a privilege and a pleasure to have gotten to "know you" through Bella and I'm very grateful that she's shared such a precious part of her life. It has certainly reminded me of my social duty to recognize, share, and nurture the potential in this around me. I hope that I may too have such a significant influence on someone's life.
>
> Thank you for reminding me to stop and appreciate our potentially profound effect on the world around us.

Mentoring tip: Help youth hold on to their bold dreams as you work together at small, achievable, and memorable action steps.

Week 28

MENTORING REFLECTIONS

It is no exaggeration to say that a strong, positive self-image is the best possible preparation for success in life.

—Dr. Joyce Brothers

DAY 1: CREATE A PERSONAL PHOTOGRAPH

An important mentoring role is to encourage your mentee to develop a positive, personal mental photograph of themselves that accompanies them throughout the day and night. As they learn how to do this, it determines how positive their self-image is, and how high their self-esteem is.

Therefore, we continually look for the positive moments in our relationship with our mentees to help them feel valued.

Authors Barry and Carol St. Clair[1] wrote: "When we value something, we honor it, love it, hold it in high self-esteem! What we live for and think about is what we value. A value is a quality, object or person that we look at and say, *that is important*."

When our mentees no longer value themselves, they could easily enter a downward spiral of behavior which could start with expressions of disappointment. These feelings could lead to further states of mind: discouragement, then despondence, then despair, and finally defeat, which could end in tragedy.

The way pro-active mentors deal with such situations could inspire mentees to achieve something truly worthwhile in their lives.

Never forget that as long as there are negative influences in society your mentee remains in high risk situations.

---

1. St Clair, *Ignite the Fire*.

Mentoring tip: Use stories to inspire, encourage, and motivate your mentee to fulfill unrealized dreams.

DAY 2: SIX TIPS TO ENCOURAGE ADOLESCENT MENTEES TO ACHIEVE GOALS

Young lives develop in a positive and new direction when mentees know how to set and achieve realistic, measurable, and achievable goals.

Here are six tips a mentor can pursue to inspire and motivate their mentees to achieve their goals, all of which I use when I mentor adolescents.

1. Make an effort to get to know your mentee before they set goals. Timing is everything. Establish trust and confidentiality. This will enhance the goal-setting process. In a case where, understandably, this groundwork is not possible, tread softly with goal setting, until you feel you have a better connection with your mentee.

2. Start with easy seven-day goals that are specific, measurable, realistic and achievable. Examples might be: record homework in a diary each day; eat breakfast; get up ten minutes earlier on school or work days; or undertake a chore or duty in the home.

3. Give regular feedback on goal achievement, with a specific focus on your mentee's *efforts*, which is critical to inspire and motivate them.

4. Encourage your mentee to take small action steps. Motivation often comes from dissatisfaction at not achieving a certain level of performance, and a desire to do better next time, rather than from the goals themselves.

5. Continually revise and revisit the goals with your mentee, and remain flexible. As lives change, goals may need to change, especially if new opportunities arise.

6. Look for performance, and not perfection. Let your mentee focus on the question: "How do I rate compared to who I see myself capable of becoming?"

Mentoring tip: Encourage your mentee to develop a personal photograph of themselves in the future, and to hold on to it in their minds and hearts.

DAY 3: SHARE STORIES DURING THE MENTORING JOURNEY

Adolescents love story-telling, especially when the stories are true. They appreciate mentors who share life experiences, as these can motivate and inspire them in different ways.

When the mentor shows the mentees how they can create their own stories simply through non-threatening, getting-to-know-you discussions, much is achieved.

Here are some topics you can discuss with mentees.

- What would you suggest are the important cultural values, types of behavior, and other aspects of your culture I should be aware of? Tell me about them, as I would like to understand your culture better.
- What are the features you like and dislike about your school, work, or further training?
- How important do you think your schooling, or education is to prepare you for your future career?
- What sort of music do you enjoy? Why? Who is your favorite singer, or group, or composer? Can you share their music with me?
- Which particular places of interest would you would like to visit? Why these places?
- Which specific sports, or cultural activities do you enjoy? Tell me about them.

You will find that, when most mentees respond to non-threatening questions like these, a discussion moves to a deeper level, and your connection with your mentee consolidates.

Mentoring tip: You establish a positive trust base on which you build your mentoring relationship when you connect with your mentee.

DAY 4: GOLDEN TIPS FOR AN EFFECTIVE MENTOR

I have often been asked how I would describe an effective mentor of young people.

There are certain guidelines from mentor training, and mentoring research I have undertaken over the years, that effective mentors follow diligently. These mentors "always" seek to make a positive difference in a young person's life.

Consider these quick tips, a check list if you like, to ensure you genuinely encourage your mentee to reach their potential.

> *A*lways aim to fulfill your potential.
> *N*ever hit, humiliate, or abuse your mentee.
>
> *E*njoy mentoring with a sense of humor.
> *F*lexibility gains respect.
> *F*amily values are "always" nurtured.
> *E*fficiency and thorough planning always pay off.
> *C*reative spirits change the world.
> *T*eamwork builds positive communities.
> *I*nspire your mentee at every opportunity.
> *V*isionary mentors educate for the future.
> *E*xcellence creates positive achievers.
>
> *M*otivate positively.
> *E*ncourage, empathize, affirm, and unconditionally care for your mentee.
> *N*urture and mold your mentee as a unique being.
> *T*ry to be firm, fair, and consistent, and never lose your sense of humor.
> *O*ffer constructive criticism always.
> *R*ole models who are positive people of influence live a healthy and balanced lifestyle.

Mentoring tip: The ripple effect of your mentoring relationship can transform society. Pass on your passion for mentoring to your mentee.

MENTORING MOMENTS

A couple of colleagues and I accompanied a group of students aged between sixteen and eighteen years of age on an overseas hockey tour.

Simon, who would later that same year earn selection for his country's national under-nineteen hockey team, acknowledged that he had much to learn.

Mentors can never underestimate the power of the interactions we have with youth. I am always surprised and left feeling humble. Simon's note to me after the tour highlights the importance of being available to youth.

Thank you for the excellent coaching you provided throughout the duration of the tour. Many boys commented on the very high standard and on your ability to motivate the side. Naturally, I must thank you on a more personal level for being available to talk to and for helping with my rather "nervous" captaincy. From the start you made it quite obvious that you were there to help me and, although that may seem very natural to you, it was something I valued greatly.

Mentoring tip: Always confront youth honestly, directly, and sensitively as this will show how much you care.

Week 29

MANAGING TIME EFFECTIVELY

Every job is a self-portrait of the person who did it. So, autograph your work with excellence.

—Author unknown

DAY 1: THE TOP FIVE MISTAKES IN MANAGING TIME

A powerful contribution mentors can make in a mentee's life is to coach them how to manage their time effectively. This is an area I find myself covering very early in almost every mentoring relationship.

Time management specialist Don Wetmore[1] has highlighted the top five mistakes most people make when their management of time is poor. I have adapted these very slightly for mentors of adolescent mentees. Each point creates a wonderful point of discussion with our mentees.

1. We start our day without a plan of action.
2. Our work area is messy, which means we waste significant amounts of time as we look for things. This leads to a loss of focus.
3. We do not take appropriate breaks, or move away from our work area to have something to eat and drink.
4. We lose the healthy and balanced lifestyle which affects our emotional, spiritual, and physical health, and our relationships with family and others.
5. We do not have sufficient sleep—nine hours *every* night for most adolescents.

---

1. Wetmore, *KISS Guide*.

Mentoring tip: Model the art of caring and taking time out to encourage your mentees to achieve their dreams.

DAY 2: USE TIME APPROPRIATELY

One area I continually work at with adolescents is the effective management of time. Once they improve their management of time skills, you will see positive developments occur. Encourage your mentees to identify different qualities of time, and to adapt their behavior to suit each one.

Here are some useful strategies which I have used successfully in mentoring relationships, and which are collated from considerable research.

- During *peak performance hours*, the brain functions at maximum level. Mentees can focus on the areas that require a high level of concentration. For example, they can revise for a test or exam, or work through a tough problem-solving task.
- Certain times are more *creative*. During these times encourage your mentee to let their ideas flow, as they are thinking clearly. They could write or design something, pursue a hobby, or read something of interest. The challenge is to stay motivated for study, or to pursue the development of a life skill.
- *Off-peak hours* cause fatigue. These times can be more constructive than many young people appreciate. For example, they can use these times to file, or write notes, carry out chores at home, or do whatever administrative work is required.

Mentoring tip: Work with your mentee to find creative solutions to the challenges they face, and you teach resourcefulness.

DAY 3: UNDERSTAND STRESS

People of any age face stressful situations at various times. Your mentee may be under great pressure (real or perceived) from parents, teachers, work colleagues, and peers to perform academically, to fulfill specific tasks, or to participate in certain activities. Many adolescents do not know how to handle such pressures. They allow themselves to become highly stressed and, as a result, may burn out, or give up. Your mentee may process some of these thoughts:

I get sudden panic feelings.
I feel anxious and wound up.
I have a strange sensation as if something awful is going to happen.
I keep focusing on worrying thoughts.
I get agitated feelings like butterflies in my stomach a lot.
I can't sit still and feel relaxed.
I feel restless and must be active!

If you detect signs of stress during a conversation with a mentee, begin a process to develop the skills to move forward and handle stress positively. If you are concerned with their behavior, however, liaise with the program coordinator, another mentor, or someone else working with youth. You can collaboratively work out a coordinated strategy. Effective management of time strategies will definitely help.

Mentoring tip: Interact frequently with your mentee. Take an open, less judgmental stance, and express optimism and confidence in your mentee.

DAY 4: MENTORING: A UNIQUE PROCESS

I remember the day Sofia approached me in my office at school.

"How can I help you, Sofia?" I asked.

"I want you to mentor me. I need help with my planning and organization. Last year I had five hours sleep most nights. I pushed myself so hard to achieve my academic goals and make my parents proud. I achieved all my goals, distinctions in all subjects, but I don't want to live like this anymore. In fact, I am not going to live like this anymore and that's why I need your help."

There it was. One simple question I ask most times when young people speak to me: "How can I help you?" The mentoring process is unique to every mentee.

In Sofia's case, she needed to express her agenda, her needs, and her priorities. My role was to do my best to empathize with her situation. She was clearly feeling anxious and stressed about her situation. She reset her goals, which were no longer aimed solely at academic achievement. She determined to lead a healthy and balanced lifestyle for the final nine months of her school career.

Sofia achieved all her academic goals at the end of that year. She told me that, with the exception of about three evenings, she had slept for a minimum of nine hours every night, and could see what a difference that made to her life. She developed a regular exercise pattern, followed a healthy diet, moved away from negative friends, and adapted her relationship with her parents. The most memorable moment occurred about half-way through our mentoring journey, when, with a big smile on her face at our weekly meeting, Sofia said: "I cannot remember when last I was as happy as I am now."

Mentoring tip: The greater your affinity with your mentee, the easier it is to resolve apparent conflicts.

MENTORING MOMENTS

Youth have different needs because they are unique. This is clearly shown in comments written by fifteen-year-old students at the conclusion of a nine-month school-based mentoring program.

> "He has helped sort through my life and make right decisions when it comes to work related things. Very awesome person. Really been good with him."

> "She helped me gain self-confidence, realize what I wanted to do in the future, how I was going to get there and has helped me achieve my goals."

> "She told me things I just wanted to hear."

> "Helped find the jobs I like . . . talking about jobs."

> "I now understand what I want to do in life . . . I enjoyed it all."

> "She has opened my mind to the opportunities and still has more I'd love to learn from her. She took me to a career psychologist, showing me what I am best at. She has helped open my mind . . . it is a good program."

> "She has helped me become more confident in myself and I hope that I have made a positive impact on her life as well. I wish her all the best . . . talking about each other's lives, resolving issues and having a good laugh. I liked everything. I think it was a great idea. Thank you for allowing me to have this experience."

Mentoring tip: Guide, encourage, and motivate youth to set realistic, measurable, and achievable goals which are consistent with their values.

Week 30

MOTIVATE MENTEES

> Grace, the divine quality of grace, is goodwill, friendliness, favorable regard, extravagant loving-kindness.
>
> —William Edwy Vine

DAY 1: MAKE A MENTEE FEEL GREAT

Author and commentator G.K. Chesterton wrote: "The really great person is one who makes everyone else feel great." This is a wonderful message for any mentors as it embraces the spirit of mentoring.

As a great mentor, here are some strategies to make your mentee feel great.

- Apply what your mentee learns and experiences to everyday life.
- Translate your mentee's life experiences into learning opportunities, and identify resilient qualities wherever possible.
- Identify with the community at large, and learn how to be of service to others. Encourage your mentee to become a positive change-agent.
- Let your mentee make a few growing mistakes when they learn new skills, as long as the experiences are not life threatening or potentially harmful.
- Praise each small success of your mentee at every opportunity. One implicit mentoring rule should be to make at least one compliment every time you meet.
- Share with your mentee how you attained your current job. What training was required? Is it the job you aimed for in secondary or high school? What other jobs have you done since your adolescence? What

life experiences did you gain from them? What are your strengths? How were these identified? Share your story.

Finally, be encouraged, by these thoughts shared by the National Mentoring Partnership (MENTOR), one of the global youth mentoring leaders:

> Disconnection, an underlying factor in our society, hits young people the hardest. Mentoring is connection. By getting involved with mentoring, you are helping ensure a bright future for your community and your neighborhood. You will be giving, but also receiving something in return—a big smile, laughter, energy, and a fresh way of looking at the world around you.

Mentoring tip: Effective mentors know themselves, and are prepared to go the extra mile.

DAY 2: HOW TO RECOGNIZE A NURTURED MENTEE

Effective mentors develop a positive friendship with their mentees. One way to evaluate your effectiveness as a mentor is to look out for the following signs of nurturing which mentees will display.

- Mentees have a sense of belonging.
- Mentees have a better perspective of themselves.
- Mentees have a sense of hope for the future.
- Mentees have a stronger sense of self-worth.
- Mentees have a feeling of significance.

Psychologist Jennifer Fox Eades[1] stated: "Children who are high in self-control do better in school, have better self-esteem, fewer problems with anger, and better relationships." These are also positive signs of a mentee who is in a nurturing mentoring relationship.

Mentoring tip: Mentoring is about knowing the art of timing—when to be silent; when to allow your mentee to stumble and fall; when to reach out and help them along.

DAY 3: CREATE CIRCLES OF SUPPORT

One important life-lesson I share with adolescents over and over again, is that it is a strength and not a weakness to ask for help. So, it is important

---

1. Fox Eades, *Celebrating Strengths*.

to talk about other people my mentee trusts, and who they can approach for encouragement and support when we both agree that the time is right.

While it takes courage and requires certain communication skills to approach others, it is also an important aspect to build resiliency. My mentee and I work on the development of the communication skills required for this task.

I become more comfortable in the knowledge that my mentee and I are part of a wider circle of support as this relationship building process gets under way. It is an important stage of our life journey, most especially for adolescents.

If we are honest, we all need mentors in our lives.

I think back to the mentors I had as a teenager. These people definitely helped shape my life and spoke to the potential in me that I could not see at the time. I think of Bruce, Anthony, Colin, David, Joe, John, and Michael, who were either teachers, coaches, or my school principal—some of whom I have written about in the "Mentoring moments" messages in this book. Some of these people continued to mentor me into the early years of my career, and beyond. They unselfishly invested their time in me. My way to repay them is to keep the spirit of mentoring alive, and to pass on the mentoring baton to the next generation.

Mentoring tip: Good corporate and public policy is investing in youth through a mentoring relationship. Spread the message.

DAY 4: DEFINE SUCCESS

Youth mentoring expert Kristie Probst[2] stated that a key role mentors can play in the life of adolescent mentees is to help them define success "as making choices that open the doors to numerous options for their future, rather than choosing to engage in activities that can close doors."

This involves talking about what is possible, and the goals that *can* be achieved. Mentors avoid being caught up in limitations and obstacles. The well-known statement comes to mind: turn the obstacles into opportunities.

I always share with youth one of my life mantras: *there is a solution to every problem*. Then we discuss possible solutions, and collaboratively create positive and flexible strategies.

---

2. Probst, *Mentoring for*.

Kristie suggested: "At its best, a successful mentoring relationship can provide a young person with critical support and opportunities for growth that he or she may not be receiving in life."

One of the best and most meaningful definitions of "Success" I have come across, and which I also share with youth, is that written by legendary basketball coach John Wooden[3]: "Success is peace of mind that is the direct result of self-satisfaction in knowing that you did your best to become the best you are capable of becoming."

Mentoring tip: Effective mentors persist. They show empathy, and continually mirror the strengths they see in their mentees.

MENTORING MOMENTS

How many teachers or coaches were your mentors during your school years?

During my final year of school our cricket team went on a brief interstate tour. We travelled in cars and stopped off to visit a retired History teacher nicknamed "Wilkie." He welcomed us into his home with open arms. "Wilkie" had been my History teacher for at least a year, so he knew me and had some idea of my capabilities.

I wrote a thank you letter to "Wilkie" on behalf of the team after we had returned home from the trip. His reply and special insights, which embrace much of the *spirit of mentoring*, remains one of my treasured school memories.

> I'm delighted you plan to schoolmaster. There is no finer profession for those who enter it as a vocation; and you will be an asset indeed, if I may presume to say so—first and foremost in terms of character and example, and second, apart from the form room, which can and should be fun, you will be valuable out on the sports field.

Mentoring tip: Seek to focus on the health and wellbeing of youth when communicating with them, rather than on yourself.

---

3. Wooden, *Wooden*, 170.

Week 31

FAMILY AND SUPPORTIVE NETWORKS

> A mentor is an older, more experienced person who seeks to further the development of character and competence in a younger person.
>
> —Professor Uri Bronfenbrenner

DAY 1: SEIZE THE MOMENT

Mentors must remind themselves from time to time, that one of the main purposes of their mentoring relationship is to create opportunities for healthy discussions that will result in lifelong learning for their mentees, and assist them to develop positive characteristics that can be permanently stored in the developing brain.

Look to explore opportunities to move your mentee out of their comfort zone and expand their horizon. Be a committed, consistent, and non-judgmental cheerleader.

At the same time, be sensitive to your mentee's family situation, as you are ultimately responsible to them for all that occurs in your mentee's life as a result of the mentoring journey. This is a massive responsibility, but have faith in your mentee as well, especially when things might be wobbly in your mentee's family life.

How well I recall a discussion about positively resolving conflicts with a group of students. The next day the father of one of those students came to see me to thank me for that discussion. His son had returned home from school the previous afternoon, to discover his father and mother in a heated disagreement. Their son paused proceedings and shared what he had learnt about positively resolving conflict situations earlier in the day. His parents got into their car, drove off, went to a quiet place to talk, and positively resolved the issues they had been arguing about.

I was reminded that day never to underestimate the positive impact a young person can have within a family environment.

Mentoring tip: Watch yourself flourish when you observe your mentee grow as a result of your productive, fun time together.

DAY 2: THE IMPACT OF A FAMILY ON A MENTEE

I have found over the years that working with adolescent mentees is considerably more challenging when the family does not function well.

I have seen "drone parents" who get in the way and protect their children because they have their own agendas for their children. They contribute to the emergence of a "powderpuff" generation of young people who will struggle in an increasingly entrepreneurial, innovative world, where one might have to risk failure to achieve dreams.

When I wear my education and mentoring hats, as well as reflect on my years of experience working with youth, I can see the potential damage a parent's suffocating love will cause, but I have to pull back, as I am unable to save a child, or rescue a family.

So, all I do is try and sow many positive seeds of hope, and trust that one day the young person will remember our discussions, find another mentor, and start to put into action some of their own ideas without fear of failure or perfection.

Often, I observe how absent, or inadequate, or incompetent parenting results in the escalation of the mentee's antisocial behavior. Brain research states that this can ultimately lead to delinquency and chronic criminal behavior.

Brain researchers also state that severe and chronic stress in an adolescent's life can be linked to physical and emotional abuse, though the good news is that deficits might not be permanent because of the plasticity of the brain.

I have always consulted professional mental health practitioners whenever I have worked with mentees in many of the situations shared in this Mentoring Minutes message.

Mentoring tip: Model patience, especially with regard to your mentee's attitudes and mistakes. Remind yourself on occasions of the different feelings you experienced as an adolescent.

DAY 3: MENTEES: A PRODUCT OF A VARIETY OF COMMUNITIES

I often share the importance of the mentoring quality of empathy when volunteer mentors meet their adolescent mentees during the early stages of the mentoring journey.

While mentors continually learn how to mentor from the heart, and to be authentic and vulnerable at appropriate times, they can also try and gain knowledge about the world in which their mentee lives.

What are the family dynamics? What can you learn about the school your mentee attends? What is your mentee's neighborhood like? Which social media platforms grab your mentee's attention? What TV programs does your mentee watch? What music does your mentee listen to? Is your mentee linked to a sport club, or youth group, or faith group within their community?

As you gather the answers to questions like these, you gain a deeper understanding of who your mentee is, and how deeply these influences impact that young life.

Let your mentee observe you model the power of the spirit of mentoring through your interactions with them. Examples include a willing commitment to the relationship, consistently turning up for the meetings, expressing genuine kindness and concern towards your mentees, and being that non-judgmental cheerleader.

A final word from mentoring expert Thomas W. Dortch Jr.[1]: "Mentoring is a life-affirming cycle that has the power to heal the wounds and divisions of our society and that expands every time two people touch each other's lives as mentor and mentee."

What specific gift or gifts do you bring to your mentoring relationships?

Mentoring tip: Coach your mentees how to put excuses aside so they can deal positively with problems, or issues.

DAY 4: MENTORS HAVE FUN

I have found over the years when I mentored adolescents that one of the great gifts I contribute to the relationship, other than encouragement, is a sense of humor. I laugh at myself, as well as coach my mentees how to laugh at themselves, and to have fun in a positive way, without making fun of others. This becomes more important as young people engage in conversations

---

1. Dortch Jr., *The Miracles*, 195.

with their peers on social media. "How would you feel if you received that text?"—a simple question that can lead to a wonderful discussion about the responsible use of social media.

When Dawn shared a particularly painful family experience she had endured at the hands of her dominating father, she cried, reflected, and shared deep feelings. Then she reminded herself of her capabilities, and her goals, and thanked me for listening. I mostly listened, asked open-ended questions, and helped her to unpack her thoughts and feelings during a time of confusion in her life.

Towards the end of our conversation she said she felt much better. She thanked me for my care and encouragement. One of her final comments, with a cheeky smile on her face, was directed at herself.

When I started to mentor Dawn, she found it difficult to laugh at herself, and took life far too seriously for one so young.

As we connected and shared our life stories, her mindset changed and, six months later, despite a painful experience, the smile was there and her inner and outer beauty shone through. She smiled through her eyes, so I knew she was authentic—a magical mentoring moment.

Dawn felt lovable and capable as she developed into a more confident and resilient young woman.

Mentoring tip: Understand that time can mean different things, at different times, to different people, your mentee included.

MENTORING MOMENTS

Sometimes peer mentors can impact our choices in ways beyond our imagination. Ignatius Kusiak was one such person as chair of the parents' association of the school where I was the principal.

We respected and empathized with one another and our respective roles. Ignatius led from the front, and was unafraid to roll up his sleeves and do the dirty work, especially with regard to organizing the annual fundraising school fair.

Ignatius and I felt that we needed a new fee structure to see the school continue on its growth plan. With the support of the School Board, we spent many hours developing different models. Ignatius had the practical knowledge and financial experience, and I had the crazy ideas. We persevered, laughed lots, stumbled along together, until we finally developed a model that was approved by the Board and celebrated by the parents.

My relationship with Ignatius reminded me of the importance of teamwork, humility, the power of goal getting, courage, perseverance, and never being afraid to chase a dream.

A special season alongside a significant role model and friend in my career journey.

Mentoring tip: Expect youth to change, and understand that positive change occurs when the best strategies to reach their potential are agreed upon.

Week 32

FEEDBACK IS IMPORTANT

> Start doing what is necessary, then do what is possible; and suddenly you are doing the impossible.
>
> —St Francis of Assisi

DAY 1: MENTORS' WORDS TO INSPIRE

Some more thoughts volunteer adult mentors shared with me about what they would have liked a significant adult to say to them when they were teenagers, to encourage you to think carefully about how and when you affirm your mentees.

The power behind these short sentences is significant, especially when shared by an authentic mentor.

"I know that you can do it!"

"Pursue your dreams and never give up on that prize."

"I think you're really brave being able to cope on your own."

"Keep doing what you're doing. Stay optimistic."

"I know you are capable of achieving anything you set out to do in your life."

"You have an optimistic and very positive outlook on life."

"Believe in yourself. You have all the capabilities."

"People need to see and read what you have to say."

Every message communicates a word of "hope" and encouragement. During the mentoring journey it is important for mentors to pause on occasions, and reflect on the quality of the messages their mentees hear in their interactions with their mentors.

Mentoring tip: Every gesture, facial expression, and action sends a message to your perceptive mentee—make sure you build positive self-esteem.

DAY 2: THE ART OF A MENTORING CONVERSATION

The face to face conversations during a mentoring relationship are transformative as the mentee's brain develops. Brain research reveals that, by the age of fifteen, most young people's reasoning abilities are developed. They are happier and healthier when they are in supportive relationships. When we add humor to our conversations, a positive growth mindset is stimulated.

The more our mentees have meaningful conversations, the more they develop their capacity for critical thinking and self-awareness. When I do not agree with my mentee, the fact that I respectfully listen and do my best to understand their viewpoint, means that I help my mentee learn how to think more clearly and critically about the community in which they live.

My mentee learns how to stay in touch with their feelings and thoughts, and how to express themselves in an environment in which they feel safe and secure. These conversations are unlikely to take place with their peers, or their parents, or most teachers.

Youth often hide their true feelings out of a fear of disapproval or rejection.

Mentoring tip: Effective listening skills involve mentors using silence while mentees share feelings, and mentors do not know what to say.

DAY 3: GENERAL MENTORING TIPS

Volunteer adult mentors who communicate with adolescent mentees continually reflect on how positive and meaningful the relationship is.

Here are some helpful points to reflect on.

- Look for opportunities to provide constructive and effective feedback.
- Timing is important: know when it is your turn, as mentor, to "listen." Listen to what is *not* being said, as well as to what *is* being said. Once you have listened, "ask" if you can recommend a possible way forward, a person to contact, a book to read, a website to look at, or a YouTube clip to watch.

- As the formal mentoring relationship draws to a close, reach consensus on the way ahead. For example, perhaps you and your mentee may agree that less regular, ongoing contact would be helpful. Some research stated that the most positive results come from a mentoring relationship of at least two years' duration, probably because the longer timeframe allows a stronger connection, and the establishment of a deeper level of trust.
- Never be afraid to try different strategies and focus on what Daniel J. Siegel[1] calls: "structure with empowerment, or, how we can support adolescents whilst also allowing them to find their own voices."

Mentoring tip: Great mentors accept their mentees with unconditional and non-judgmental care.

DAY 4: MENTORS MOTIVATE

In the early stages of the relationship the mentor drives the relationship. The mentee tries to find their way, and decides whether or not the mentor can be trusted. As the relationship develops, the mentor steps farther back and allows the mentee to drive the relationship. So, it is all about empathy and the mentor knowing when to let go, and how to move at the pace of the mentee. This is significant in the establishment of a meaningful, developmental mentoring relationship.

Fifteen-year-old students reflected briefly on their mentoring experiences and wrote these comments. Note the variety of responses. Every mentee is unique.

> "Helped me with job opportunities e.g., work experience."

> "She has helped me write my resume. She organized work experience. Good rapport."

> "She has helped me with a lot of things . . . having someone to talk to."

> "He has been there if I needed to talk . . . make it last longer."

> "She has taught me to control my anger and shown the importance of a good career."

---

1. Siegel, *Brainstorm*, 33.

Mentoring tip: Take an open, non-judgmental stance with youth. Express optimism and confidence in them, and share messages of hope.

MENTORING MOMENTS

Most students enjoy participating in non-threatening activities facilitated by an organized and empathetic trainer.

These comments from seventeen-year-old peer mentors who were introduced to some key aspects of mentoring, were responses to a question which asked them to highlight the most important lessons they gained from the day's activities.

> "Don't be shy and bored or they will feel boring with you; try to do lots and opening your mind, even your heart to someone is good for friendship; good jokes can make others happy even one week later."

> "I've learnt about teamwork, how to be a leader and a follower in a group of people; the understanding of others was encouraged and activated today, after being together for one year!!; competition is not the most appropriate way to judge a person; friends seem to be more important than I really thought—it made me also think back to my family."

> "Had great fun and enjoyment; realized that people think I'm lively. Discovered what others thought about myself; the different ways that a person can listen and respond to a conversation."

> "That I am not the most important, but everyone is equal; a mind to share with others; trust; patience; understanding."

These activities promoted the spirit of mentoring, while encouraging students to participate fully in a self-empowering, and self-discovery journey. Youth have so much more to offer, and more competencies than we often realize.

Mentoring tip: Establish positive and collaborative relationships with youth. Build a network of support around them.

Week 33

COACH STRENGTH-BASED STRATEGIES

> All people feel better and do better when you give them attention, affirmation, and appreciation.
>
> —John Maxwell

DAY 1: SKILLS OF A GREAT MENTOR

Volunteer adult mentors are special people who want to identify their mentee's strengths, and see their mentees reach their potential.

Here are ten of the most important skills and attributes of a great mentor—which I have collated after years of research—for the creation of an effective mentoring partnership.

1. Have a positive outlook on life and on others. Display that unconditional love, so you can disapprove of your mentee's behavior, while still caring for them.

2. Display the qualities of honesty, humility, efficiency, and a clearly defined set of values, and remain a collaborative team player.

3. Possess excellent communication skills. These include the ability to empathize, listen, understand, reflect, clarify, validate, encourage, question, and offer constructive feedback.

4. Model the ability to set realistic, measurable, and achievable goals, or tasks.

5. Display imagination, innovation, and creative thinking to inspire your mentee to fulfill their potential.

6. Display patience, especially with your mentee's attitudes and mistakes, together with perseverance. *Never* quit on your mentee.

7. Be approachable, flexible, teachable, and open-minded. This includes sound skills for the management of time.
8. Able to encourage your mentee to appreciate how self-discipline and restraint are the doorways to freedom.
9. Display the ability to see solutions as well as obstacles. Remain proactive in your approach and thinking.
10. Show a consistent refusal to accept verbal abuse or physical intimidation.

Mentoring tip: Be relaxed, authentic, empathetic, and trustworthy, with a great sense of humor, and watch your mentee soar.

DAY 2: HOW TO COACH RESILIENT CHAMPIONS

The spirit of mentoring involves the development of positive relationships with mentees during some of the most confusing times of their lives.

Effective mentoring sees the mentor become the cheerleader of a resilient champion, their mentee.

Here are some of the qualities and strategies one can adopt to develop a positive relationship with adolescent mentees, all of which I have used over many years.

- Show empathy at all times, and meet your mentee's emotional safety needs as best as you can—this takes time.
- Express consistent, non-judgmental, and unconditional care.
- Be an inspiration.
- Be trusting and trustworthy.
- Be empowering, respectful, and compassionate.
- Coach mentees to take ownership of the fact that they have the power to create their own realities.
- *Always* be a good listener.
- Provide a mirror and model of what can be attained.

Mentoring tip: Help your mentee make sense of the world. Be the best cheerleader you can be.

DAY 3: BUILD A WEB OF PROTECTIVE FACTORS AROUND A YOUNG PERSON (1)

A significant contribution a mentor can make to the life of a mentee is to build a web of protective factors or characteristics around the young person that will reduce the negative impact of stressful situations or problems, and so develop resiliency.

Some ways a mentor can do this would include the six strategies—highlighted by resiliency experts Nan Henderson and Mike Milstein[1]—which I will share in this, and the next Mentoring Minutes message. When combined, they result in the development of positive self-concepts, connection to school, improved academic results, respect for authority, and a more resilient young person. I can vouch for this from my mentoring, teaching, and coaching experiences.

1. *Provide unconditional care, support and encouragement.* Let mentees hear the message *"You matter!"* Catch them being good, and acknowledge their *efforts*.

2. *Increase bonding.* Strengthen the connections between mentees and positive adults and peers; and between mentees and any positive social activity—sports, art, music, writing, dance, community service, reading, or learning. Mentees with strong and positive bonds are less likely to be involved in high risk behaviors.

3. *Set clear and consistent boundaries.* Mentees need clear and consistent rules, or boundaries—family rules and norms, school policies and procedures, community laws and norms—within which they are encouraged to fulfill their potential. These must be clearly spelt out and consistently enforced. Negotiate with your mentees over the boundaries and enforcement procedures (and consequences) with a caring attitude, so they gain a sense of ownership, and receive the authentic message that they are a valued community resource.

Mentoring tip: When you observe your mentees feel good about themselves, and become more self-confident and resilient, celebrate the positive mentoring journey.

---

1. Henderson, *Resiliency in Schools.*

DAY 4: BUILD A WEB OF PROTECTIVE FACTORS AROUND A YOUNG PERSON (2)

In the previous Mentoring Minutes message, we considered three strategies a mentor uses when mentoring, and which are likely to lead to the development of high self-esteem, with many positive developmental spin-offs.

Here are three further strategies. We observe some wonderful personal development, including a growth mindset, as our mentee becomes more resilient when we follow the six strategies.

1. *Teach life skills.* Some key life skills are cooperative skills, healthy conflict resolution skills, resistance and assertiveness skills, communication skills, problem solving and decision-making skills, and healthy stress management to enable our mentees to cope with life's challenges.

2. *Set and communicate high expectations.* High and realistic expectations are effective motivators. For example, we can authentically share words like these with our mentees: "*I believe in you!*"; "*I know you can do it!*"

3. *Provide opportunities for meaningful participation.* Give mentees responsibility as you encourage opportunities to solve problems, make decisions, plan, set goals, and help others. Allow them to share power with adults in real ways. See them as resources rather than as passive objects, or problems. Encourage mentees to join school and youth committees, peer programs, and youth related programs.

Mentoring tip: Walk in your mentee's shoes from time to time, and sometimes feel the blisters.

MENTORING MOMENTS

These comments written by mentors of fifteen-year-old students at the conclusion of a nine-month school-based mentoring program, highlight the diversity of mentoring experiences.

> "Helped [him] focus on priorities and actions taking you closer or away from your goals. Better time management awareness. Some public speaking tips. A wonderful experience. I really enjoyed it and got a lot from it."

"I enjoyed the training, meeting other mentors from varied areas of the community, the matching process and getting to know my mentee. I introduced the idea of graphic art to [him], an area that he is very interested in and didn't know was available as a career path."

"I believe I encouraged [her] to see herself in a more positive light, which is good. However, I did not manage to encourage her enough so that she plans on staying longer at school."

"She is having more emotional days than in the beginning, which I see as her identifying her thoughts and how and why to deal with them. Her marks and organization have improved. [I enjoyed] watching the growth of a young community member; learning how to deal with varying emotions . . . occasionally her emotional rollercoaster rides concerned me—that I was losing my way with her—*but* Robin always set me on the right way again."

"I feel that I have made a small difference in her life. She is a very shy girl who maybe didn't have a lot of confidence in herself. She is slowly gaining confidence and starting to believe in herself. I enjoyed seeing her grow over the last few months even though it was small changes."

Mentoring tip: Always strive to accept every young person with whom you connect; look for their strengths and praise every effort.

Week 34

MORE CHALLENGES

When opportunity comes, it's too late to prepare.
—John Wooden

DAY 1: A SAFE HAVEN

One of the critically important roles mentors play in the lives of mentees is to provide a safe space, or haven for them to share sensitive issues about themselves, their families, teachers, friends, and others with whom they interact on a regular basis.

How you respond, how you listen, and the interaction you have with your mentee, becomes a way you share your values and perspectives on life. Never underestimate how powerful these moments are.

Generally, adolescents are quick to dismiss parental advice. However, more often than not mentees appreciate the guidance and encouragement of their mentors when they connect with them. You have the knowledge and life experiences which their peers lack. Those peers also deal with personal issues, and everything is that much tougher when parents, and other adults are scarce.

So, take your time as you try and understand the influences which impact your mentee's life during the early stages of your mentoring relationship. Keep your eyes wide open, and listen carefully, especially for what is not being said. Ask questions that do not invade your mentee's privacy. They will share when they are ready and believe you will listen and not judge them.

Mentoring tip: Your mentee is worthy of the investment of your life energy. Do you believe this?

DAY 2: HOW TO HANDLE TRUANCY AS A MENTOR

I have experienced a few occasions when a young person I was informally mentoring started to play the truancy game. I sat down with these young people, and we shared the purpose of education, their hopes—and often doubts and fears—and dreams. I listened, and listened, and listened while they processed and unpacked their experiences. And then, in every single case, they set new and achievable goals, and we connected into a formal mentoring relationship for a season of their lives.

In some cases, I linked them up with counsellors and other adults for additional support and encouragement.

Here are a few tips from my personal experiences, which also overlap with experiences from other mentors. Remember that each instance of truancy, or dropping out of school, for example, will be different.

- Establish a friendship with your mentee.
- Share ideas about the economic and social costs of dropping out (of school, work, or further training, as applicable).
- Discuss the long-term options for your mentee. What options will remain open if they leave school before they are ready to do so, or terminate a job without adequate notice, or give up a training course without completing it?
- Consider adopting a seven-step strategy to work through with your mentee:
    1. Stop. Think about the problem. Discuss it.
    2. What are some positive choices?
    3. Choose *one* of those options.
    4. Write it down.
    5. Put it into action within a given time.
    6. Arrange a time for follow-up together.
    7. At the follow-up, discuss how the chosen option worked. Celebrate the small victories as they are achieved.

If you are linked to a youth mentoring program, *always* discuss this matter with program staff.

Mentoring tip: Remind your mentees that the choices "they" make in life are likely to define their circumstances.

DAY 3: SET BOUNDARIES

Mentors continually remind themselves how important it is to set clear boundaries during the early stages of the mentoring journey. Research states that most adolescents, especially boys, appreciate these clear boundaries.

Boundaries include an agreement about when and how mentors and mentees will communicate with each other; when and where they will meet; how often and for how long each time; and what sort of activities they will do together. Clarify the role of the mentor and how long the mentoring journey will last, especially when you are linked to a youth mentoring program.

Chat about accepted language and behavior in a friendly, non-threatening, and social way. For example, my mentees know that I do not appreciate coarse language (swearing), yet they also know there might be times when they explode in the safety of our relationship, and the odd word will flow from their mouths. That is okay, as I know such emotional outbursts are also linked to the developing adolescent brain.

However, they respect my values, and we create strategies to take our relationship to deeper levels as we get to know one another.

My mentees know from day one that their health and wellbeing are important to me, and that when they speak to me, they are the most important people in my life during that time.

Mentoring tip: Effective mentors know the limits of their strength and abilities, though always strive to reach their potential.

DAY 4: AN ADOLESCENT'S TEN MENTORING REQUESTS

Some years ago, sixteen-year-old Jessica Manning[1] shared some thoughts about how adolescents could be treated by adults. Her thoughts remain relevant, and contain some great tips for mentors as they help their mentees work through challenging times.

1. *Responsibility*: give us a chance to prove to you that we can be responsible.
2. *Respect*: treat us like you would like to be treated.

---

1. Manning, *New Zealand*.

3. *Trust:* do not judge us just because we are teenagers . . . Not all of us are bad.
4. *Give us a chance* to make mistakes, learn from experience, and to explain our opinion, or our side of the story.
5. *Care:* let us know you care.
6. *Support:* we need support; we need to be reassured we are doing the right thing.
7. *Understanding:* listen to what we have to say and understand that we have stresses and problems too. Although they may seem insignificant to you, they are big to us. Being a teenager is not easy: understand this.
8. *Balance:* do not leave us totally alone. We need you to catch us if we fall.
9. *Give us praise* when we do things that are good, or make the right decisions.
10. *Freedom:* it may be hard, but let us go. We have to leave our own footprints and make our own decisions and mistakes. Part of growing up is finding out who we are, what we value, and what we need as a person. Only we alone can make that journey.

Mentoring tip: Focus on your mentee's health and wellbeing, rather than on yourself.

MENTORING MOMENTS

Dave Hiscock was my History teacher for the final two years at school. Early in my final year, Dave called me aside in the school grounds and, in his blunt, no-nonsense manner, informed me that I was likely to fail if I did not step up my academic efforts.

Dave had coached me sport earlier in my high school career, and encouraged me in other ways. He clearly saw my potential that I could not envision.

I took up the challenge, though. My best result in my final public examinations was History. I graduated with a degree majoring in History, and became a History teacher.

When I emerged from hospital at the end of my cancer-related journey at the age of eighteen, Dave surprisingly visited me at home. Eighteen months later he invited me to be a student tutor in his boarding house for the final two years of my university studies.

During these and subsequent years—I would teach History at the school for two years—Dave mentored me. He coached me how to connect with testosterone-fueled young men. He shared History teaching thoughts and resources, and modeled how to make the subject relevant in young lives.

Shortly before he died of cancer in his retirement, I wrote him a note to tell him that the differentiated teaching style he had used to teach me, and which was becoming popular in the school where I was teaching thirty-five years later, showed how far he was ahead of the time, and how privileged I felt to be taken under his wing all those years ago. His daughter later told me that he had noticeably perked up for a while when he read that note. He died a few days later—my mentor, my friend.

Mentoring tip: Know the limits of your strengths and potential as you strive to become the best role model when you connect with youth.

Week 35

MENTORING REFLECTIONS

A mentor is someone who allows you to see hope inside yourself.
—Roberto Blizzard

DAY 1: HOW A DEVELOPMENTAL MENTORING RELATIONSHIP BENEFITS A MENTEE

Researchers state that there are noticeable and significant benefits to the mentee when the mentor and mentee work together to enjoy the mentoring relationship. The mentor travels at the pace of the mentee, which usually requires patience.

Here are five of the most significant benefits to the mentee from a positive and meaningful relationship which have been collated from youth mentoring research.

1. Mentees have a clearer direction with regard to career opportunities and choices.
2. Mentees become goal getters, which often leads to improved academic and non-academic performances.
3. Mentees develop stronger and more positive relationship building skills.
4. Mentees develop higher self-esteem.
5. Mentees display a greater sense of responsibility, reliability, and resilience.

Mentoring expert Thomas W. Dortch Jr.[1] states: "This is the time when you must show genuine interest in your mentee. Find out about the young

---

1. Dortch Jr., *The Miracles*, 114.

person's interests and dreams. Talk about setting goals. Most important, express your satisfaction with seeing your mentee grow and develop, no matter how small the changes. That is the best way to demonstrate that you care."

Mentoring tip: Effective mentors build character more than skills.

DAY 2: AN EXPERIENTIAL JOURNEY

I remember reading an interesting mentoring experience.

One of the most important skills this mentor polished and refined was effective or active listening. He had to remind himself more than a couple of times, when he was meeting with his mentee, to leave his own ego at the door. This was the time he set aside to invest in the life of a young person, to encourage, care, coach him, and set goals together. Above all, the mentor had to *listen* to his mentee, to discern how his mentee felt, and to hear what his mentee might not say. This involved learning how to ask non-threatening, open questions, show great sensitivity and empathy, and look for moments when he could genuinely affirm his mentee's efforts.

This mentor said he had enjoyed a wonderful experiential journey, as he learnt so much more about himself while in this developmental relationship with his mentee.

Most of my mentoring relationships with young people echo this mentor's experience, and I continue to learn.

Mentoring tip: Effective mentors know themselves, and are prepared to go the extra mile. They never seek to replace their mentee's parents, or caregivers to become the most important person in their lives.

DAY 3: BE THAT MIRROR

I came across a wonderful quote attributed to Ken Keyes Jr.: "A loving person lives in a loving world. A hostile person lives in a hostile world: everyone you meet is your mirror." This is a great quote to help mentors understand the importance of their modeling during a mentoring experience.

Mentees connect with their mentees within a few weeks when they experience a non-judgmental, encouraging, and supportive cheerleader who consistently turns up to meet them. They might not receive unconditional care from anyone else. The value of at least one significant non-parent adult in every adolescent's life should never be underestimated, although some youth mentoring research states that at least three significant adults would be preferable.

Adolescent brain research also highlights the importance of a significant adult in the lives of youth during the turbulent and confusing adolescent years—someone to keep them calm, identify their strengths, and help them process the variety of challenging issues they deal with. Wise mentors steer their mentees into a space where the mentees come up with answers, or make suggestions to resolve their issues. These times are immensely satisfying for a mentor who observes first-hand the importance of the mentee's self-empowering journey.

Dennis Saleebey[2] the editor of *The Strengths Perspective in Social Work Practice* (2001) wrote:

> People are more motivated to change when their strengths are supported. People I have interviewed who have left gangs, recovered from alcohol and other drug addiction, made it successfully through college despite a childhood of abuse, or overcome other significant traumas have told me the same thing. "The people who helped me the most were the ones who told me 'what is right with you is more powerful than anything that is wrong with you,'" a young man who successfully completed college despite a childhood of living in one foster care after another told me.

Mentoring tip: View your mentees positively. Observe the way they start to view themselves and change their attitudes towards parents, teachers, peers, and other people.

DAY 4: THE JOYS OF MENTORING

Have you ever thought about what would give you joy as a mentor? Or, if you have already mentored young people, what gave you joy?

When I reflect on my mentoring experiences, one thing that always gives me joy is literally watching a young person grow before my eyes, often in quite unexpected ways.

Their body language becomes more assertive as self-confidence develops; they become more independent, or self-reliant thinkers; they start achieving goals, and come to appreciate that it is possible to have, and to chase dreams, and they take ownership of their inner and outer beauty.

One mentee said to me, "I knew you were a good friend when you reassured me, I'm beautiful just the way I am; when you helped me through

---

2. Henderson, *Resiliency in Action*, 185.

my heartache, cheered for me along the way and laughed with me over nothing at all."

What also gives me joy is when my mentees come to appreciate that there are people who care for them, and genuinely want to walk alongside them for a while. Twenty years later a mentee sends me a note expressing their thanks for a life-changing moment we shared, and I had no idea how important that particular moment was in that young life at the time.

Mentoring tip: Great mentors encourage their mentees to always exercise excellence.

MENTORING MOMENTS

When I first met thirteen-year-old Sean I detected a sensitive young boy. Sean's father had died when he was much younger, and Sean was struggling to find his way with the strong support of his understandably protective mother.

Over the years I spent time with Sean, encouraged his goal setting journey, explored ways for him to utilize his love of music and culture, and his interest in drama and writing. He became an empathetic student leader, and would later create a successful career for himself as a writer.

When I left the school, Sean was sixteen. He shared these thoughts with me.

> I think [the school] has given me more than I can realistically grasp. For even being at [the school] I am indebted to you. You have provided me with a privilege and, both directly and indirectly, taught me most of what I know. Without writing "Odes to Mr Cox," or getting too sentimental, I would simply like to say thank you. . . . I hope we don't lose touch.

Mentoring tip: Mentoring involves investing time and energy in young lives as a non-judgmental cheerleader.

Week 36

THE DIFFICULT CONVERSATIONS

The kids who need the most love will ask for it in the most unloving of ways.

—Author unknown

DAY 1: RESOLVE CONFLICTS WITH AN ADULT

If your mentee tries to resolve a conflict with an adult, the adult is likely to have the edge, as your mentee may not

- be as articulate as the adult;
- be as skilled at controlling feelings;
- be self-aware enough to understand the reasons behind their feelings or behaviors;
- have enough life experiences to appreciate the consequences of some actions or attitudes;
- appreciate the value of conciliatory gestures or apologies.

For these reasons, a mentor plays a critical role in unpacking the issue with their mentee, even role-playing the adult involved in the conflict with the mentee. This helps and encourages the mentee to have the courage to resolve the conflict with positive outcomes.

This event can be a significant life-changing moment in the mentee's life. The mentor needs to be sensitive, patient, non-judgmental, and display an overabundance of empathy.

Mentoring tip: Great mentors care and believe in their mentees to insist that they strive to reach their potential. This is the heart of mentoring.

DAY 2: POTENTIAL PITFALLS FOR COLLABORATION

When mentors discuss *collaboration* as a possible style to resolve conflicts, it is worthwhile to help mentees understand some reasons why "collaboration" might not work.

- The problem was not defined clearly.
- Emotions were not handled first before an attempt was made to try and resolve issues.
- The brainstorming process did not include evaluation or clarification.
- The finer details were not worked on.
- There was no follow-up to make sure that the agreed action steps were taken.

I have found, over the years, that most adolescent conflicts are linked to their relationships with family, friends, or other adults. The steady, guiding hand of a non-judgmental mentor can significantly assist the development of a young person's relationship building skills.

Mentoring tip: Help your mentee envision new horizons and possibilities, which will probably involve a move out of their comfort zone.

DAY 3: CHOOSE THE MOST APPROPRIATE PROCESS TO POSITIVELY RESOLVE CONFLICTS

Mentors contribute significantly to their mentees' ability to maintain peace of mind when they coach them how to apply key skills to resolve conflicts with a positive mindset. Never underestimate the effect that these skills can have on a community. Your mentee will probably pass those skills on to peers, families, work colleagues and others, as they follow your example, and become role models in their communities.

Different situations call for different conflict resolution methods, including mediation, or restorative justice in some cases. For example, a case where a smaller student is being bullied by a bigger student would require a different approach from a case that involves an adolescent's disagreement with a teacher, or a clash of values between a parent and child. The methods typically used by different cultural groups involved in a conflict are also relevant. Respectfully find out as much as possible about their approaches.

Mentoring tip: Encourage your mentee to become excited as they learn about the world in a safe and secure mentoring environment.

DAY 4: RESOLVE A CONFLICT BETWEEN A MENTOR AND A MENTEE

If you, as a volunteer adult mentor, are involved in a conflict with your adolescent mentee, here are some useful guidelines, which I tend to follow—thanks to the work of Gael Lindenfield[1]—to help you work through the issue with your mentee.

- Make the first move and suggest you have a talk.
- Be the first to offer an apology if this is warranted.
- Show respect for your mentee's feelings and position, with a genuine desire to listen to their point of view and, if possible, make a positive comment or observation.
- Encourage your mentee to express any negative feelings towards you before you offer any criticisms.
- Describe the problem in an objective and non-threatening way.
- Ask questions, or sensitively make suggestions (based on any assumptions you make), which may help your mentee understand less obvious causes that may be behind the conflict. For example, there could be issues like loneliness, the generation gap, jealousy, boredom, or confused communication.
- Help your mentee articulate arguments and suggestions in an assertive style if they lapse into aggressive behavior or are too passive.
- Demonstrate how to back down with good grace from arguments when these have proved to be illogical, unfair, or out of date.
- Show your mentee ways to make amends when they hurt someone, or destroy something.
- Draw the negotiation to a positive conclusion when either of you becomes too tired or too emotional to continue.
- Facilitate the final summary, in which you outline any new agreement, or decisions, and spell out what you both may have learned and

---

1. Lindenfield, *Success*.

positively gained from the conflict. Arrange a follow-up time to make sure that you and your mentee are happy with the decisions taken.

Mentoring tip: Always consult and involve your mentee when you consider what you will do together.

MENTORING MOMENTS

Pat was quiet, a little dreamy, though had many competencies that required nurturing and encouragement. He lacked self-belief initially, yet learnt how to set goals that stretched him, and to explore his areas of interest.

He grew in confidence and achieved much. He shared these thoughts with me as he reflected on his final year at school.

> Thank you for the wonderful couple of years with you in [the boarding house]. Your sensitivity, concern, and solid spiritual guidance have helped make my latter three years, this last one in particular, a great time of growth and enjoyment for me. Getting to know you and to appreciate the principles by which you so firmly stand, while working as a [student leader] under your leadership, has brought with it so much that I'll be sure to cherish in the years to come. Thank you once again for all your goodness to me.

Mentoring tip: Always affirm the life of a young person, and encourage their unique potential to become the best they can be with the support of those they trust.

Week 37

CREATE MEANINGFUL RELATIONSHIPS

You were born an original. Don't die a copy.

—John Mason

DAY ONE: PIONEERING MENTORS

When we contemplate the mentoring journey, we look at mentors as pioneers. They venture into unexplored space as they meet a stranger, their mentee, seek to create a connection, and provide a place of safety and security in which to develop the relationship.

Mentors encourage their mentees to step out of their comfort zones and explore new possibilities. This journey is important in the development of the adolescent brain. These mentors are the wise guides on the side who sow seeds of hope, and develop a vision of what might be in the future.

Mentors focus on character growth ahead of skill development. They encourage their mentees to chase their dreams, and not to quit when the going gets tough. At such times the mentor reaches out their hand, and helps the mentee reposition themselves on life's path—a pat on the back, a smile, a positive word of encouragement—and displays all the signs of the significant non-parent adult who never quits.

This pioneering spirit is rewarding and satisfying as mentors observe a young person strive to reach their potential.

Educator and adolescent brain expert Sheryl Feinstein[1] offered a word of encouragement: "Promote a sense of mastery in our students. As the brain is naturally social and collaborative, providing opportunities for

---

1. Feinstein, *Secrets*, 144.

personal interaction will engage students in the learning process and give them an incentive to keep participating."

Mentoring tip: Seek the small victories and watch your mentoring relationship blossom.

DAY 2: HOW TO CREATE A MEANINGFUL MENTORING RELATIONSHIP (1)

A meaningful mentoring relationship should be regarded as a journey that takes time, and includes asking open-ended questions when we communicate with our mentee.

In discussions with your mentee, invite them to answer with more than a brief *Yes* or *No*. Use open questions that begin What, Why, When, How, What or Who? Notice the difference in the following examples:

Closed questions	*Open questions*
Did you appreciate that?	What did you appreciate about that?
You must have felt excited when . . .	How did you feel when . . . ?
Did you feel intimidated when . . . ?	Who intimidated you and how did you . . . ?

A key aspect of your communication with your mentee is timing. Timing helps you communicate effectively. Here are some useful tips.

- Choose the best time to communicate.
- Think before you speak.
- Allow space for silences, especially while your mentee reflects and considers whether or not to share more information. Silences might make you feel uncomfortable. I have found on a number of occasions that a prolonged silence led a mentee to take the discussion to a deeper level. They often use the silence to pluck up the courage to share more about themselves, or an issue they are confronting.
- Ask for a moment to reflect when you have been listening and have not framed a clear response. This is a great skill to model to your mentees.

Mentoring tip: One of the most teachable moments your mentee will experience is when they ask you a question which they might never have asked someone else.

DAY 3: HOW TO CREATE A MEANINGFUL MENTORING RELATIONSHIP (2)

Empathy is an important quality for a mentor to display in the creation of a meaningful mentoring relationship. Try to put yourself in the shoes of your mentee to gain some understanding of how they feel.

Sensitive listening means you try to feel what your mentee feels. You may find it helpful to think of a time when you felt a similar way, or were in a similar situation. Be a perceptive listener and pay attention to the entire person with whom you communicate.

Here are some helpful ground rules for effective listening.

- Do not interrupt.
- Do not change the subject or move in a new direction.
- Do not rehearse in your own head.
- Do not interrogate.
- Do not teach (unless you are assisting your mentee with academic work, for example).
- Do not give advice (except on certain appropriate occasions, and then with the permission of your mentee).
- *Do* reflect back to your mentee what you understand and how you think your mentee feels.

Keith Davis shared a powerful lesson all effective mentors can take to heart: "Nature gave Man two ears but only one tongue, which is a gentle hint that he should listen more than he talks!"

Mentoring tip: Great mentors are people of character who are trustworthy, consistent, and stable.

DAY 4: HOW TO CREATE A MEANINGFUL MENTORING RELATIONSHIP (3)

The messages that mentors communicate non-verbally to their mentees are often more important than their verbal responses. Examples of non-verbal cues are

- tone of voice;
- facial expressions;

- gestures;
- eye contact;
- posture.

Most research I have come across states that for any message, 38 per cent of the impact on the receiver is derived through tone or inflection, 55 per cent through body language (appearance, or gesticulation), and only 7 per cent through the words said. Therefore, your tone of voice and body language have the potential to be highly persuasive communication tools.

In this digital age coach mentees non-verbal behaviors, as these are behaviors social media platforms cannot adequately teach.

Do not stand up and pace around, or make yourself appear to be some menacing, autocratic, and tyrannical authority figure when you communicate with your mentee.

Keep your eyes at the same level as your mentee where culturally appropriate.

Watch your mentee's body language. Your mentee, like you, can send powerful non-verbal messages that give added meaning to the spoken word.

Listen more than you speak to your mentee. Do not interrupt or become judgmental. Only offer advice, solutions, or suggestions once your mentee has thought through possibilities under your guidance.

Effective listening involves listening beyond the words to the truth of the situation. A good listener is a warm, friendly person, who cares about others, has compassion, is basically kind, and listens with patience and interest. Continue to practice acting like a mirror. Reflect back how you think your mentee feels as you summarize comments.

Mentoring tip: You provide an opportunity for your mentees to clarify and get in touch with their feelings and thoughts as you listen to them.

MENTORING MOMENTS

Unfortunately, not all mentors can work in partnership with parents or caregivers of mentees. When one is able to do so, results can be amazing. That is the best way to describe my surprise when I received this note from Chloe's father after I had spent a few months guiding and encouraging sixteen-year-old Chloe through some challenges.

Although we haven't formally met, I "know" you through discussions I've had with my daughter Chloe. I just wanted to say a very quick thank you for all the support, direction and encouragement you've shown Chloe during the whole leadership selection process and more particularly, the past few months. We are very fortunate that she has a very good relationship with [two colleagues] and will seek them out for assistance from time to time, but I know you have also helped her out significantly, and we are thankful for that.

Chloe has had a couple of other personal issues to deal with of late and has begun to feel a little isolated from some of her peers, but your input has definitely helped her maintain a healthy, positive perspective (of both herself and where she "fits in" among her peers) regardless of the outcome. From our point of view, self-belief and a positive outlook are still some of the most valuable personal traits we can aspire to, and you consistently encouraged her along these lines. Again, I thank you kindly for what you have done with Chloe. It is greatly appreciated.

Mentoring tip: Remind youth that the choices they make in life are likely to define their circumstances and how they progress on life's journey.

Week 38

ALL ABOUT GOALS

They may forget what you said, but they will never forget how you made them feel.

—Carl W. Buehner

DAY 1: SEEK . . . STEPPING STONES

One of the great gifts a mentor gives a mentee is an investment of time and energy to coach and guide them how to set specific, realistic, measurable, and achievable goals, how to evaluate the goal getting journey and, as this experience is enriched, how to stay focused, and chase their dreams.

Help them to create small action steps, or stepping-stones, to achieve each goal they set, and genuinely celebrate every small victory.

Coach youth how to deal with setbacks and failure, because your major focus as a mentor is on character development.

You experience great pleasure when your mentee steps out of their comfort zone, attempts something, fails, and then meets with you to tell you what they have learnt from the experience. They share how they will take these lessons and use them to achieve their dreams. Inspirational moments, that is for sure.

You certainly do not want your mentees to live with any regrets.

Mark Twain advises: "Twenty years from now you will be more disappointed by the things you didn't do than by the ones you did do. So, throw off the bowlines; sail away from the safe harbor. Catch the trade winds in your sails. Explore. Dream. Discover." That is a wonderful way to describe an effective mentoring journey.

Mentoring tip: Effective mentors know how to prioritize, do not fear failure, and are flexible.

DAY 2: ENCOURAGE MENTEES TO ACHIEVE THEIR GOALS

When adolescents learn how to set and achieve goals, they develop potentially life-changing skills with the non-judgmental support of their mentor.

Here are some topics linked to goal setting which can form part of the discussions between mentors and mentees.

- Make a list of anticipated obstacles to achieve a goal. Work out ways to turn these obstacles into opportunities for further personal growth.
- Consider all skills, information, knowledge, resources, and help from people and organizations your mentee might need to achieve a specific goal.
- Remind your mentee that the goal getting journey must have flexibility written into it to allow changes if the mentee's personal circumstances change.
- Do not let goal setting become the master of your mentee's life. Goals must bring mentees real pleasure, satisfaction, a sense of achievement, and be fun. They must be aligned with the mentee's developing values base. If this is not happening, revisit the goals.

Mentoring tip: Watch your mentees grow before your eyes as you teach them how to develop the confidence to make personal choices.

DAY 3: EXAMPLES OF ACHIEVING GOALS ON THE MENTORING JOURNEY

Every mentee is unique. This is clearly shown in some examples of goals achieved by mentees during mentoring relationships that I know about. All these mentees acknowledged the important role the mentors had played in their personal development.

- A mentee's grades in one academic subject improved from 28 percent to 50 per cent over a six months period.
- A mentee worked on lifting weights at a gym. The mentor used this exercise to teach goal setting. They developed a great mentoring relationship.
- A mentee obtained a part-time job with the help of a mentor.

- A mentee and mentor visited shops in a shopping mall, and picked up job application forms as they visited different shops. The mentee gained a job that same day, and achieved their goal without having written any goal-setting steps. The connection between mentor and mentee provided a foundation to build on for the remaining months of their mentoring journey.
- A mentee worked at aerobic fitness, as she had been invited to be a bridesmaid at a friend's wedding later in the year. She lost weight and improved her self-image. Her mentor determined this from her mentee's increasingly positive body language, and attitude to life.

Mentoring tip: Coach your mentee to take on tasks and challenges which will make them proud of themselves. They develop high self-esteem as they do so.

DAY 4: POSITIVE GOAL GETTING STRATEGIES

The goal setting journey between a mentor and a mentee always has its challenges, partly because of the unpredictability of adolescents during a time of significant physical and emotional development.

Mentors are discouraged from spending money on their mentees, so they do not become a mentee's ATM machine. There are always exceptions as can be seen in this story of an overweight adolescent mentee, Gary, who wanted to exercise, yet lacked the motivation to do so.

One day Gary went fishing with his mentor, and the mentor's young family. As it was Gary's birthday, the mentor gave him a gift voucher. When he arrived home after the outing, the mentor received a phone call from Gary to say that he that he had already bought fishing gear with the gift voucher. In the months ahead, Gary gained in self-esteem, improved his academic work, and increased his fitness through all the exercise involved with fishing.

However, to place things in perspective, here are four examples of positive mentoring relationships where no money was spent by the mentor.

1. A mentee, after encouragement from their mentor, attended the homework center at school. This led to academic improvement and increased self-esteem.
2. A mentor drew up a goal-setting strategy on the computer with his mentee, who was interested in computers.

ALL ABOUT GOALS

3. A mentee committed to read one novel a week to improve his English with the encouragement and support of his mentor.
4. A mentee joined the local library with the help of their mentor.

Clearly, some of the goal setting tasks are significantly more challenging than others. Much depends on the space the adolescent occupies during the mentoring journey and the environment in which the mentee lives.

Mentoring tip: Share your goals with your mentee, and you motivate and inspire each other.

MENTORING MOMENTS

I love training volunteer adult mentors because they are keen to invest their time mentoring our youth to reach their potential. Some mentors shared these comments about the value of the training program prior to embarking on a mentoring journey with an adolescent mentee. They share useful tips to encourage all mentors.

"Not to put words in mentee's mouth."

"The importance of realistic goal setting and time management."

"My reactions to conflict, communication style etc.—to remember that I have an "automatic" [reaction to certain situations] and not let this affect the mentee."

"Ok to be human—to embrace that I don't know all the answers and being vulnerable provides an opportunity to grow."

"Managing conflict, how to be a friend rather than another authority figure."

"Be thankful for what you have; the need for effective communication; my lack of goal setting."

"Vulnerable—listen more; don't try to predict the outcome. I am not being judged."

Mentoring tip: Sow the seeds of the spirit of mentoring in the lives of youth, in the hope that they become positive people of influence who will one day powerfully impact the global community.

Week 39

DEVELOPMENTAL RELATIONSHIPS

A real friend is one who walks in when the world walks out.
—Walter Winchell

DAY 1: NURTURE RESILIENCY IN MENTEES

Well-known Australian psychologist Andrew Fuller[1] stated: "Resiliency is the ability to bungee jump through life. It's not that you avoid the pitfalls and difficult times, but when they do happen you have skills to get out of it. It is as if you have an elasticized rope around your middle that helps you bounce back."

Nurturing resiliency begins with a positive, non-judgmental attitude, expressed verbally and non-verbally. Through this attitude you convey the following message to your mentee:

> No matter what your problems are at the moment, no matter what you have done in the past, I believe in you. I want to encourage you to develop all your positive qualities, gifts, and talents. As you do so, you will appreciate that you can bounce back from the hassles, setbacks, and other obstacles you will face throughout your life.

Aim to be a role model who walks the talk because, as you integrate ideas and attitudes into your interactions with your mentees, you nurture resiliency, and build self-esteem both for yourself and your mentees.

Mentoring tip: Think about the people who affirmed you, acknowledged your gifts, talents, and self-worth. How did they impact you? Now go out and do the same for your mentee.

---

1. Fuller, *Raising Real People*.

DEVELOPMENTAL RELATIONSHIPS

DAY 2: COACH SOCIAL SKILLS AND VALUES

Mentors have a wonderful opportunity during the mentoring journey to coach and teach social skills and values, and have discussions that mentees might never have with their parents.

Here are a few ideas, all of which I have used when I mentored young people.

- Coach and discuss respect for the opposite sex, and other gender issues your mentee is interested in, and about which they would like more information.
- Take opportunities to talk with your mentee about issues such as fairness, right and wrong, consideration for others, and responsibility.
- Discuss the importance of boundaries. You, therefore, protect your mentee from situations they may not be able to deal with.
- Be protective and angry on your mentee's behalf in the face of injustice—for example, if your mentee is bullied, or put down by a teacher or another adult, or unfairly discriminated against.
- Discuss assertive, aggressive and non-assertive behavior, and any other pertinent issues if you watch a movie, TV, or a video with your mentee.
- Accept your mentee's feelings and communicate *your* feelings with integrity. Coach different methods to control and express feelings. Help your mentee to articulate their feelings. Watch your mentee's body language to ascertain their level of assertiveness, or aggression.
- Encourage your mentee to always do what they believe is right, and support their values.
- Consistently model basic values and standards, and *make sure you are in the relationship for your mentee.*

Mentoring tip: One way to win the hearts of your mentees is to tell them they are needed and valued.

DAY 3: COACH PRACTICAL SKILLS

When mentors coach their mentees practical skills during the mentoring journey, they encourage the development of a positive growth mindset, assertiveness, and resiliency.

Here are five ways to assist you.

1. Help your mentee to take responsibility for tasks that someone else may have done previously. Teach skills for performing those specific tasks.
2. Help set specific, measurable, realistic and achievable goals with a clear action plan. Celebrate achievements together. Encourage your mentee to do things that make them feel good. The satisfaction of creating something, completing a project, or achieving a personal goal is one of the best ways to build self-esteem.
3. Give practical assistance, support, and feedback to your mentee. Effective feedback facilitates change. Do not lecture, insult, ridicule, label, exaggerate, patronize, use sarcasm, induce guilt, or try to force your mentee to do something. Do not dominate the conversation. Be shockproof and transparent. Allow time.
4. Allow your mentee to make mistakes in an environment that is as safe as possible—both emotionally safe from destructive criticism, and physically safe from danger to self, or others—and help your mentee learn from them.
5. Teach your mentee how to cope with longer periods of effort before any rewards are evident—delayed gratification.

Mentoring tip: The only time a great mentor will get in their mentee's way is when the mentee is on the way down!

DAY 4: MAKE SENSE OF CONFUSION

Adolescents go through one of the most confusing times of their lives with regard to physical, emotional, and social development. Their brains are at a critical stage of development, so they need—and value, though might not express this—significant trustworthy adults in their lives, understanding and supportive parents, and a non-judgmental mentor or coach.

Here are some simple tips to guide youth through these times of confusion.

Assist your mentee to see other options. A mentee often does not see the exits when on a wobble. You can make sense of the confusion with firm countering statements.

- "You will," counters, "I won't!"
- "You can," counters, "I can't!"
- "You're great," counters, "I'm no good!"

Assist your mentee to hear the following messages within themselves:

- I like myself.
- I can think for myself.
- I am lovable.
- I matter, and my voice matters.
- I am capable.

Assist your mentee to clarify a problem. Ask your mentee questions like:

- "What is wrong?"
- "How does it make you feel?"
- "What are you going to do about it?"
- "How can I help?"
- "What can we do about it?"

Finally, and most important of all, continually work at your own wellbeing. Reflect on the following questions:

- Do I have a healthy and positive self-image?
- Am I modeling a caring and optimistic view of the future?
- Am I continually focused on the development of my own self-esteem? (high self-esteem is contagious.)

Mentoring tip: Mentoring is not about fixing families, or children. It is about moving alongside a young person, and having fun together.

MENTORING MOMENTS

Mike Thompson was an experienced teaching colleague who thought outside the box, had a strong sense of social justice, and was a wonderful role model. He was talented in many areas, and unafraid to speak his mind no matter the cost.

During my days as a school principal, I had envisioned setting up a non-racial school in Cape Town in an area that would attract students from a variety of socio-economic areas.

Mike and I were teaching in different schools, in different parts of the country. I always looked up to him as a visionary, and had considerable respect for his education philosophy.

I wrote to him and shared my vision. I also shared some of the obstacles I knew I would encounter. Mike's response carries a message of encouragement and hope for all mentors: "Keep trying, Robin. Without dreams, the world comes to a halt."

In the end, I could not gain permission from the local council to use that land, and so the dream was never realized. However, Mike guided and encouraged me to persevere, and I will always be indebted to him for having the willingness to share his wisdom and experience with a "dreamer."

Mentoring tip: You gain increased wisdom, character growth, greater empathy and a deeper understanding of youth issues from the time you spend with your mentee.

Week 40

BUILDING SELF-CONFIDENCE

> Don't walk in front of me; I may not follow. Don't walk behind me; I may not lead. Just walk beside me and be my friend.
> —Albert Camus

DAY 1: A PORTRAIT OF ASSERTIVENESS

A "Wow!" moment in a mentor's life is when they reflect on the mentoring journey, and observe how their mentee has become a more assertive person.

Here are some assertive signs collated from global research.

- They have the ability to cope with life's challenges.
- They display all the signs of a positive self-image, positive self-worth, and developing self-confidence.
- There are signs of honesty, trustworthiness, the ability to speak their mind, sensitive expressions of feelings, strong bonds developing, as well as mutual respect in their relationships.
- They show a great sense of independence, and are able to make choices, even when these are a challenge.

Mentoring tip: Encourage a sense of curiosity, good manners, and a considerate nature in your mentee, and you leave a mentoring legacy.

DAY 2: WHAT IS SELF-IMAGE?

Self-image is an individual's mental photograph of themselves which they take with them day and night. It sums up the person's answer to the question: "What do I think about myself now?"

The answer may encompass a number of areas, which include physical appearance, emotional state, personality, intelligence, social roles, and creativity.

How an adolescent mentee perceives the combination of factors such as those mentioned is significant. For example, mentees who are happy with their achievements, yet do not feel loved, may eventually experience low self-esteem.

Likewise, mentees who feel loved, yet are hesitant about their own abilities, may feel poorly about themselves. Healthy self-esteem results when the right balance is achieved.

I am thankful to those mentors who spoke to the potential they could see I had when I was a confused adolescent and could not see what they envisioned: remarkable people with insight and wisdom, many of whom have been mentioned in the "Mentoring moments" messages in this book.

Mentoring tip: Carry the flame of the mentor's spirit: an unseen, affirming influence, combined with positive energy.

DAY 3: STUMBLING BLOCKS TO EFFECTIVE COMMUNICATION

Mentors can reflect on the times they experienced a breakdown in communication when they were teenagers. This helps to avoid possible barriers during the early stages of the mentoring journey. What were the stumbling blocks that led to each breakdown?

As a mentor, do your best not to practice those same attitudes which became barriers between you and adults during your adolescent journey.

Some of the common stumbling blocks teenagers have mentioned, when questioned about such barriers, are: ordering; directing or commanding; threatening; moralizing or preaching; lecturing; judging; diagnosing; prying; name-calling; nagging; avoidance; sarcasm; glassy-eyed listening, and continually bringing up the past when the young person tries to move forward positively.

The timing of conversations is important, as is the courage of mentors to speak the truth sensitively and empathetically when required. Mentoring expert Thomas Dortch[1] writes:

> Sometimes, mentoring requires tough love. You have to be willing to say no, to correct, to ask hard questions, and to speak

---

1. Dortch Jr., *The Miracles*, 52.

unpleasant truths. You might get resistance from the young person you are working with. You might get a sullen look now and then. You might even get a resentful word. But in the long run, what you will get is a whole lot of respect and gratitude.

Mentoring tip: Mentors with excellent listening skills are able to respond fully to their mentees' feelings, before they respond with facts.

DAY 4: THE IMPORTANCE OF COMMUNICATION SKILLS

One of the areas I spend some time chatting about with mentees is how to work through conflicts in a positive manner. Many of their conflicts are linked to relationship issues.

Often what lies at the root of a conflict is not so much a failure to communicate, but a failure to *understand communication* (perhaps with additional reasons in very difficult situations). For example, two parties may make a concerted effort to communicate as clearly as possible, but cultural differences or language barriers obstruct good understanding between them.

Where there is a total absence of communication between two or more parties, there is no foundation from which they can clarify positions, intentions, or past actions. As a consequence, rumors can spread unchecked.

Conversely, by developing good listening skills on an ongoing basis, a mentee learns how to resolve conflicts positively and avoid stumbling blocks to communication. Conflict resolution and communication are closely linked.

Conflict resolution expert Jennifer Akin has stated that two major techniques of conflict resolution are active, or empathetic listening, and the use of *I*-messages rather than *you*-messages. *I*-messages are concerned with communicating without placing blame, and doing one's best to understand what the other person is saying. Even where a conflict cannot be resolved, Akin noted: "making the extra effort to improve communication between the disputants is often helpful in reducing the intensity of the conflict."

Mentoring tip: Stand by your mentees whose behavior might be as a result of ignorance and stupidity, because you believe in them.

MENTORING MOMENTS

Sheila Sisulu, Raymond Louw, and Philip Putland were significant mentoring role models when I became a school principal of a newly established non-racial school—a school open to all races and cultures from day one in an apartheid South Africa—during challenging times.

Sheila's father-in-law, Walter Sisulu, had spent many years in the Robben Island prison alongside Nelson Mandela because of their opposition to apartheid. Sheila was the chair of the school Board, the wise guide at my side, whose willingness to share knowledge and life experiences provided life-changing moments for me. I spent hours talking to her. I invited her to coach me how to express a more empathetic attitude as I sought to understand the experiences of many students whose families were oppressed under apartheid policies. Sheila expressed patience and tolerance towards my—often—naïve approach to some of the issues the school faced. She stood tall alongside me when we were confronted by difficult parents. She modeled courage in the face of adversity, yet optimism and hope for the future, and possessed a wonderful sense of humor. When I met Walter Sisulu, soon after his release from prison, a selfless man who was passionate about the creation of a united South Africa, Sheila stood proudly by his side.

Raymond was a courageous journalist, a former newspaper editor and visionary who had stood tall against apartheid for many years and at great personal cost. He was the deputy-chair of the school Board, and a strong team player. His gift was the way he guided me through the problem-solving process, never sat in judgment on me, and always affirmed and respected me as a person, while supporting my decisions. Above all, he cared deeply about me, and the school, and its future.

Philip chaired the school finance committee. He had an incredible brain for figures, a wicked sense of humor, genuinely cared about me, my family and our wellbeing, and always made himself available for a chat. Philip challenged me more than any other Board member to continually imagine what might be possible, and never to fear moving out of my comfort zone with the knowledge that I had his support. In his own quiet way, he was a visionary. He would drop an idea into a conversation and often I would then explore it, look at the possibilities with him, and we would decide whether or not it was feasible at the time.

Sheila, Raymond, and Philip—three totally different and unique individuals who shared a similar passion to make a positive difference; people who enriched my life in ways beyond their imagination, and who I remain humbled to call my mentors, and friends for a season of my life.

Mentoring tip: Always seek to follow an effective mentor policy of "show and tell" when you connect with youth.

Week 41

A GROWTH MINDSET

> Don't play small. Good is not good enough. Follow your passion. Back yourself. Be yourself. Love what you do. You are capable of way more than you think you are.
>
> —GAIL KELLY

DAY 1: STRENGTHEN THE BRAIN

Daniel J. Siegel[1] points out how the work of scientists shows that adolescents can learn the steps to make their brain more integrated, and how to strengthen it. They can learn how to improve the way their mind functions. This makes their brain healthier and, as a consequence, they are more likely to enjoy healthier and more meaningful relationships.

Mentors play a significant role in this journey as they encourage and guide their mentees in the following ways:

- to actively pursue positive and enjoyable experiences;
- to develop balanced and healthy lifestyle habits;
- to enjoy positive relationships with friends and family;
- to accept responsibility for their choices and reactions to what others say and do;
- to know how they feel, and learn how to express these feelings in a responsible, and non-threatening manner;
- to convert negative experiences into positive learning opportunities.

Mentoring tip: Effective mentors confront their mentees and always demonstrate unconditional love and acceptance.

---

1. Siegel, *Brainstorm*, 18.

DAY 2: MAKE POSITIVE CONNECTIONS WITH MENTEES

Every adolescent, like their mentor, is a unique individual with special gifts and talents. There is no one specific strategy a mentor can follow to connect with their mentee.

Here are a few examples gleaned from positive mentoring relationships to encourage anyone who embarks on a mentoring journey with youth.

- Design a special certificate of congratulations for your mentee to celebrate the achievement of a goal or challenging task.
- Ask to see your mentee's last two school reports to gain an idea of how they handle school. This often results in some positive goal setting tasks.
- Introduce your mentee to at least one other person who might help by offering career advice, or the chance for job shadowing, or part-time work.
- Discover your mentee's hobbies and interests. You might find you have something in common.
- Consider a fun, written contract between you and your mentee to encourage your mentee to improve in an agreed area (while you agree to work at something as well). For example, your contract could focus on an exercise program, or an action plan to achieve some short-term goals, or a specific characteristic that needs to be worked on.

Mentoring tip: Continually remind yourself that a mentoring relationship must be a positive experience built around fun.

DAY 3: ENDING THE FORMAL JOURNEY

Many mentors are linked to community youth mentoring or school-based mentoring programs that have a specific season. Both the mentor and mentee know what the commitment is.

However, it is important for the mentor to prepare the mentee for the end of the formal journey. More life skills are taught when your mentee learns how to deal with their feelings during a time of transition.

A couple of months before the formal relationship ends, begin the discussion about the way ahead and the options your mentee has. Do your best, if this has not been discussed earlier, to make sure that your mentee has linked up with one or two other significant adults who can be added to their mentoring network. You might be prepared to continue the relationship with your mentee—many mentors do this—although you might agree to scale back meeting times.

Sometimes the mentee will be ready for the formal relationship to end. You will notice this. Your mentee might have found a job, or is finishing school, and heading off to further their studies.

Work hard to remain that non-judgmental cheerleader at all times and, as I often say to students, and try and model myself: "Finish well!"

Mentoring tip: A mentee whose mentor listens with their whole being to how the mentee feels, experiences a feeling of acceptance and flourishes.

DAY 4: WHY SHOULD ADOLESCENTS HAVE VOLUNTEER ADULT MENTORS?

Consider some comments by a variety of people to help you understand why mentoring is such a powerful gift for an adolescent to receive.

New Zealand parenting experts Ian Grant and John Cowan[2] state: "Teenagers need at least one adult in their lives to be irrationally positive about them. They need at least one person who is "in their corner"! They need to know someone is cheering for them."

Christie, a volunteer adult mentor wrote: "It's such a gift to be included in my student's life, having her call just to chat and share what's going on. Her relationships have improved dramatically over the last year with parents, teachers, peers, and me."

Finally, mentoring expert Marc Freedman[3] shared the findings of Bernard Lefkowitz after he had interviewed approximately five hundred youth from high-risk environments:

> Again, and again, I found that the same pattern was repeated: The kid who managed to climb out of the morass of poverty and social pathology was the kid who found somebody, usually in school, sometimes outside, who helped them invent a promising future. In practical terms, the presence of the understanding, concerned, yet demanding mentor transforms the meaning and quality of education.

2. Grant and Cowan, *Parenting Teenagers*.
3. Freedman, *The Kindness*, 64.

Mentoring tip: Mentors possess a genuine desire to make a positive difference in a mentee's life.

MENTORING MOMENTS

I always enjoy training mentors because we share a passion to inspire our youth to reach their potential. We pass the baton from one group to the next, and from one generation to the next.

I felt humbled to receive this comment from a program coordinator at the conclusion of a sixteen-hour experiential mentor training program. I had offered to facilitate the launch of this new program.

> Thank you, Robin, for all your mentoring time, knowledge and teaching. The guys and I really appreciated all that you did for us. I hope that we can now take this knowledge and put it to good use. Your legacy will certainly continue with us and so on with those we mentor.
>
> Coaches inspire hopes,
> nurture dreams,
> and encourage success.
> They show you that life
> means sometimes
> winning with honor . . .
> and sometimes losing with grace.
> They support the talented,
> comfort the troubled,
> and promote good character.
> (Author unknown)
>
> Mentors and coaches are everyday heroes . . . Thanks for being such a great one.

Mentoring tip: Mentors who continually speak messages of hope will nurture resiliency and a growth mindset in the lives of their mentees.

Week 42

MENTORING REFLECTIONS

Don't smother each other. No one can grow in the shade.
—Leo Buscaglia

DAY 1: A GRAFTING EXERCISE

Quite some time ago I read a wonderful analogy shared by mentoring expert Thomas W. Dortch Jr.[1]

Thomas tells the story of how a former Mayor of Atlanta Bill Campbell described mentoring as grafting yourself onto the life of your adolescent mentees as they search for meaning, direction, and purpose in their lives.

As you move alongside your mentee and graft onto your mentee's life, never forget how powerfully this experience can enrich your mentee. You graft all your personal life experiences onto your mentee's life, and those experiences of your mentors, and other positive people who grafted their lives onto you.

Remember, too, that during the mentoring journey you become the safety net for your mentee, or the anchor, the steady, strong, reassuring presence in their life.

As you invest your time and energy into the life of a young person, live in the hope that one day your mentee will pass on the mentoring baton to "their" adolescent mentee. What could be a finer way for your mentee to show their gratitude to you for all you contributed to their life?

Mentoring tip: Encourage your mentee to focus on detail, for that is where their ultimate success might lie.

---

1. Dortch Jr., *The Miracles*, 150.

DAY 2: THE RELATIONAL GLUE

I love the way mentoring expert Bobb Biehl[2] describes mentoring as: "the relational glue that can hold our generation to the last and to the next. Mentoring is the relational bridge," he goes on to say, "connecting, strengthening and stabilizing future generations."

These are powerful words and a reminder of what an awesome privilege and honor it is to be invited by a young person to walk alongside them as a non-judgmental, caring, encouraging, fun-to-be-with cheerleader for a season of their life.

This is my opportunity to give back and to make a positive difference in the life of my mentee. Perhaps my mentee will go on and change history in a powerful, and positive way. My contribution was to encourage them to chase their dreams, and to speak to the potential they might be unable to see at that particular time for any number of reasons.

It is a wonderful feeling when my mentee is vulnerable, expresses deep fears and concerns, feels able to share weaknesses, and knows that I will not judge, but cheer them on. Two people open their lives to one another and their hearts touch for a while.

Mentoring tip: As you observe and encourage your mentees to fulfill their potential, you create a legacy of hope to be passed on from generation to generation.

DAY 3: GENERAL THOUGHTS FOR THE MENTORING JOURNEY

Self-reflection is invaluable as we embark on a mentoring journey. We think about our adolescent years, the people who helped shape our decision-making, and how we reacted to specific issues and challenges.

Here are a few important points to help shape the mentoring experience.

- A great deal of what we learn about ourselves we learn from others.
- We can learn about ourselves from what others say about us, such as: you are clever, friendly, beautiful, or talented—although we do not have to accept all that people say.

---

2. Biehl, *Mentoring*, 141.

- The love of parents and family make us confident and more able to express and receive love.
- Those who have never felt loved often find it very difficult to love.
- Those who have continually been let down by adults find it difficult to trust an adult, including a mentor, as they fear being let down yet again.
- The mentoring relationship involves a commitment. Never begin the mentoring journey if you are not prepared to make the commitment.
- Many mentors have different life experiences from their mentees. There could be socio-economic, value, and family differences. Mentors adjust their expectations of their mentees as they embark on the process to discover their mentee's world. Mentors appreciate how similar or different they are, and work hard to be non-judgmental, and empathetic. Always see yourself as a cheerleader of youth, a seed sower of potentially life-changing qualities, and strategies.
- Your mentee's environment is a major factor in the total package that is your mentee. A key mentoring role is to show your mentee that other environments exist beyond their home environment. At the same time, you can assist them to learn how to cope with situations that might overwhelm them.

Mentoring tip: Always focus on the positive qualities of your mentee, their family, siblings, friends, and the community.

DAY 4: MENTORING IS COURAGE IN ACTION

Well-known American poet and civil right activist Maya Angelou stated, "Courage may be the most important of all virtues because without it we cannot practice any other virtues with consistency."

A mentor requires courage to step out of their comfort zone into the unknown, and enter into a mentoring relationship with a mentee during one of the most confusing times of their lives, while their brains continue to develop.

Well trained mentors appreciate that their role involves an expression of unconditional, non-judgmental care, and support for their mentee. This is a nurturing, motivational and inspirational role, which is unpredictable most of the time.

There will be days you need courage to speak the truth with love, and to stay present in your mentee's inconsistent life. Remember that you are unable to protect your mentee from domestic circumstances.

Through the mentoring experience and your mentee's interactions with you, that young life is self-empowered and better equipped to deal with future challenges.

Look to name your mentee's strengths because that builds resiliency and greater self-confidence.

Remember that, with your encouragement and support, your mentee learns how to adapt to changing circumstances at home, or at school, or in the workplace, and to make smart choices.

Mentoring tip: Support your mentees when they want to take risks that are not life-threatening—be a wise guide.

MENTORING MOMENTS

The group of fourteen and fifteen-year-old students I had mentored for a year as a school principal, insisted they spend time with me on my final day at the school.

We had spent time during the year talking about life in general, setting performance goals, identifying individual strengths, and enjoying many laughs.

Zoey wrote these words in a card presented to me, a humble tribute to the power of mentoring.

> This is for all the times you've stood by us, for all the times that you have made us see; for all the joys you've brought to our lives; for all the wrongs that you've made right. For all the dreams you've made come true and for just being yourself. I'm grateful. I know you've heard these words before but they always mean much more when someone else says it. In New Zealand you will face many ups and downs. Even in times of trouble think of the words you know. Everything is a challenge in life and if things aren't good, don't give up because life isn't fair! Think of all the stories you've told us how never to give up! Enjoy life in New Zealand and look for the positives in the negatives. I hope and pray that you and your family will adjust well and will share your good qualities with others so they can experience your knowledge the way we did. Let yourself be a light in the darkness and may it never go out. Good luck in the future!!

Mentoring tip: Gently, empathetically, and sensitively guide, encourage, and coax youth to believe: "I *can* do it!"

Week 43

DEVELOP RESILIENT YOUTH

> Creativity is inventing, experimenting, growing, taking risks, breaking rules, making mistakes, and having fun.
> —Mary Lou Cook

DAY 1: MENTEES WHO CAN BOUNCE BACK

Resiliency experts, Nan Henderson and Mike Milstein[1] describe resiliency as: ". . . the capacity to spring back, rebound, successfully adapt in the face of adversity, and develop social and academic competence despite exposure to severe stress . . . or simply the stress of today's world."

Mentors can help mentees develop their personal resiliency builders, otherwise referred to as their individual qualities or strengths that help them cope with stress and adversity in their lives (see Mentoring Minutes, Week 9, Day 2). Here are some helpful ideas.

- Help your mentee to discover "one" positive personal resiliency builder or strength—name it and be a supportive, non-judgmental cheerleader. Such a discovery often has flow-on effects and leads a mentee to make changes in one area, and then another. Resilience builds over time. Many of the skills related to it can be learned and promoted—"caught and taught" by the mentor, or another adult.

- Be a resilient role model. If learning is primarily a process of modeling, mentors who walk their talk display a basic operating principle of resilience work during the mentoring journey.

- Identify your individual qualities (strengths and personal resiliency builders) to develop your own self-worth and become more resilient as you face the global community's challenges.

1. Henderson, *Resiliency in Schools*.

- Remind yourself constantly that *everyone* has the ability to bounce back.

Mentoring tip: Remain an inspiration to one of tomorrow's people of influence—your mentee.

DAY 2: A SIGNIFICANT LIFE

I have written blogs and posted mentoring tips on social media platforms to encourage and enrich mentors' lives. The feedback I receive affirms my intentions.

The mentoring journey is similar—speak positively into another life and build resiliency as you identify a mentee's strengths. For a time, I focus on the life journey of my mentee. I gain enormous satisfaction as I observe my mentee literally grow before my eyes. For example, my mentee, who set a goal of nine hours sleep a night, also placed his mobile phone in another room while he slept. He told me five weeks later that the difference in his life was significant. He felt less stressed and healthier. He could focus more on his academic studies, especially after he started eating a healthy breakfast every day.

Another example was a mentee who told me what a difference regular exercise made in her life. In addition, she had chosen to stay away from gossiping and negative peers, and made sure she had nine hours sleep almost every night. I observed a more motivated, happier young woman who began to surprise herself with how much she had achieved.

And, I should hasten to add, my life is enriched by *every* mentoring experience.

Mentoring tip: Mentees experience positive self-worth and empowerment when they feel their mentors genuinely want to spend time with them.

DAY 3: FOUR KEY STRATEGIES FOR AN EFFECTIVE MENTORING RELATIONSHIP

Here are four key strategies—shared by resiliency expert Nan Henderson[2]—for the development of a meaningful mentoring relationship, with a strong focus on the development of a resilient young person.

---

2. Henderson, *Resiliency in Action*.

1. Always communicate the *resiliency attitude*. Underpin it by expressing unconditional care and support for your mentee in as many ways as possible.
2. *Continually focus on strengths* and name them specifically. Talk to your mentee about their capabilities, talents, goals, and achievements. This reinforces that your mentee is lovable and capable, which boosts their self-esteem and self-concept.
3. *Build a resiliency web* around your mentee.
    - Increase bonding, and create positive networks of support.
    - Set clear and consistent boundaries.
    - Coach life skills.
    - Provide unconditional care, support, and encouragement.
    - Set and communicate high, yet realistic expectations.
    - Provide opportunities for meaningful participation.
4. *Never give up.* Fostering resiliency takes time and depends on the establishment of a quality mentoring relationship that is reliable, trusting, and fun. Mirror the strengths you see in your mentee when they battle, in order to teach the skills required to bounce back. Resilience does not mean you or your mentee are invincible, invulnerable, or unscathed.

Mentoring tip: Always look for opportunities to see your mentees in the winning circle—that is, they work hard to reach their potential. You genuinely affirm their efforts whenever you can.

DAY 4: USE YOUR WORDS CAREFULLY

What would you have liked a significant adult in your life to have said to you when you were an adolescent?

Here are comments adult mentor trainees shared with me. While they are so simple, they remain powerful and contribute to the development of a more resilient young person.

"You really will get there in the end if you keep working at it."

"I truly believe that you will do an amazing job of it."

"I really admire the way you persevere and encourage others constantly."

"I believe in you! And you can do it!"

"You are a very special person and you are okay just the way you are."

"You have a beautiful smile and you make me very happy."

"I'm so proud of you!"

"I believe that whatever you set your mind to you will achieve. I will be your biggest supporter. I will encourage and advise you. Most of all, I will celebrate with you!"

Maybe your mentee needs to hear an affirmative word or two from you. Let the words of Nobel Peace Prize winner Archbishop Desmond Tutu encourage you: "Do your little bit of good where you are; it's those little bits of good put together that overwhelm the world."

Mentoring tip: When you help your mentee unearth their potential, you achieve possibly the greatest good a mentor can do for a mentee.

MENTORING MOMENTS

Deane Yates was a well-respected school principal in Southern Africa. He moved to Gaborone in Botswana to found the successful Maru-a-Pula school.

On his retirement Deane returned to South Africa, where he had been principal of a leading independent school prior to his move to Botswana. His pioneering spirit resulted in the establishment of a number of New Era Schools Trust (NEST) schools, and he worked tirelessly with others to raise bursaries to bring students from disadvantaged communities to the schools.

Deane also worked tirelessly to bring about the end of apartheid in South Africa. I approached him for guidance when I sought direction in my career. Later I worked closely with him as a principal of one of the NEST schools.

Deane was my mentor for three years. He modeled courage, perseverance, compassion, innovative thinking, and was one of the most selfless men I had the privilege to work with. Deane believed in me. He coached, navigated and guided me to step out of my comfort zone and advocate for a non-racial education system during the dark days of apartheid. His unwavering faith in the face of adversity inspired me on many occasions.

When I reflect on my career, and the significant impact Deane had on my life, I am grateful that I plucked up the courage to seek him out for his counsel, and am proud to call him a mentor and friend—an exemplary role model.

Mentoring tip: Those who effectively connect with mentees can set their own performance goals, have a sense of purpose, work diligently, and display a positive attitude.

Week 44

EMPATHY AND TRUST

The people who are crazy enough to think they can change the world are the ones who do.

—STEVE JOBS

DAY 1: REASONS WHY I MENTOR

It is important to reflect on why we invest our time in the lives of our youth. Here are some thoughts from different people. Let them also be messages of hope and encouragement as you seek to establish a trusting relationship.

> After years of testing, teenagers should be ready for the freedom to fly, make mistakes and find their purpose while still living within the limitations of their home. To do this they need to be given guided independence and growing responsibility.
>
> Roger Allen and Ron Rose

> Without honesty there is no truth.
> Without truth there is no understanding.
> Without understanding there is no love.
> Without love there is nothing.
> Author unknown

> Truth and love are the essential ingredients of intimacy and meaningful relationships . . . as I share who I am, so I discover who I am.
> Author unknown

Mentoring tip: Effective mentors regard their mentees as important people in their lives, so they appreciate the importance of turning up consistently for their meetings.

DAY 2: AN EVOLVING RELATIONSHIP

Mentors continually remind themselves that the mentoring relationship is a journey over a period of time, either determined by a youth mentoring program, or directly between the mentor and the mentee.

During this time never be afraid to explore new strategies, or to make mistakes. Also, remember that it is a strength and not a weakness to ask for help if you struggle with any aspect of the mentoring relationship.

The art of formal mentoring continues to evolve, especially as we learn more from neuroscience research linked to the adolescent brain. Do your best to stay in touch with the most effective practices in the youth mentoring field.

It is also important to continually remind yourself that you are a mentor, and not your mentee's parent, or caregiver. You are the trusted guide and friend who encourages and supports a young person to move out of their comfort zone, and explore new possibilities. You provide a new dimension and perspective to your mentee's relationship with adults.

Mentoring tip: Coach your mentee to develop effective planning, organization, and management of time skills.

DAY 3: MENTORS DEVELOP THE WHOLE PERSON

Mentors wear different hats at different times during a mentoring journey. Much depends on the head space the mentee is in and the mentee's environment.

Mentors aim to see continual improvement in their mentee's daily life cycle. This might include academic achievement, work, training, cultural activities, sport, or community involvement.

Indeed, it is important for mentors to encourage mentees to look beyond their own immediate teenage lives, and identify with the local and wider community to appreciate how they can be of service to others.

The promotion and encouragement of a healthy family environment built on a strong value system is equally important. This involves encouraging mentees to feel emotionally comfortable, safe, and secure. You instill feelings of positive self-worth and high self-esteem, while your mentee embarks on a memorable and life-changing journey of self-discovery and self-empowerment.

Overall, a mentor's aim is to contribute to the development of the *whole* person.

Remember that most young people are searching for identity and self-esteem. They want people to respect them as unique individuals. Their request is simple: "Give me the chance to be me and not somebody else." Often, they are unable to verbalize this clearly.

You discover how mentoring becomes a shared opportunity for learning, personal growth, and striving to reach one's potential, while you sow the mentoring seeds within a caring environment, as educator Dr. Paul Browning[1] states: "Why is care an important practice in building trust? Because when someone cares for you, you feel safe, you feel valued, you feel understood and you feel that you matter."

Mentoring tip: Great mentors are those who wish to transform the world by investing their lives in others.

DAY 4: A MENTOR: A TRUSTED FRIEND

One of the mistakes some mentors make is to try and rescue, or save their mentees from difficult personal situations. This is *never* the role of the mentor. Professionally trained people—not volunteer adult mentors—move alongside youth who deal with serious or extreme issues.

The key role of a mentor is that of the non-parent, non-judgmental, significant adult in the life of a young person. You are the encourager and supporter who expands horizons, and models what stable, secure, and meaningful relationships are like.

Never be afraid to make mistakes. If you have a positive connection with your mentee, you journey together. You have no hope of ever being a perfect mentor, though you continually strive to be the best mentor you can be. Show humility, and ask more experienced people for help if you struggle in any way.

Your mentee watches you, notices your values, observes you "walk the walk," and "talk the talk." Be yourself. Keep the fun element at the forefront of your mentoring relationship at all times.

Mentoring tip: A mentor is a good communicator—one who listens brilliantly, yet also knows how to talk well.

---

1. Browning, *Principled*, 153.

MENTORING MOMENTS

I have mentored students and adults for about forty-five years. I am still learning about myself, and how to be a more effective mentor.

Every mentor is a unique person and in a different head space. This is what makes facilitating a youth mentoring program a fascinating experience.

Here are some snapshot comments shared by mentors at the conclusion of a twenty-one-hour experiential mentor training program. Look for similarities, differences, and unique insights.

> "I still have a lot to develop, but I am on the journey and I am ok."

> "The importance of using questions to guide a child's thinking."

> "I can still step out of my comfort zone when invited to. Something I had not done for a long time."

> "I can listen, be open-minded and empathetic. I also learnt I can choose not to be these things. I'm more aware of my thoughts, feelings and actions."

> "Never think you have all the answers."

> "It confirmed my belief in my authoritarian approach—will have to work on this *honestly*."

> "To be patient; to be honest and respectful; not to judge."

> "To make sure that I know who I am and to make sure that I clear all my background rubbish before I can help anyone else as a mentor."

Mentoring tip: You leave a positive legacy when you encourage a sense of curiosity, good manners, and a considerate nature in the lives of mentees with whom you connect.

Week 45

THE POWER OF CONNECTION

> To bring up a child in the way he should go, travel that way yourself once in a while.
>
> —Josh Billings

DAY 1: THE LONGER THE RELATIONSHIP . . .

A mentor enters the life of an adolescent for a season of each of their lives. The relationship might last for three, six, or nine months, one year, or longer.

Research over the years highlights that most mentoring relationships that last longer than twelve months result in significant growth occurring in a variety of areas of the mentees' lives—much depends on the quality of the relationship. There is noteworthy growth in self-worth, which often leads to improved academic performance and a growth mindset.

Some mentees report not only improved relationships with their parents and siblings, but also a greater sense of belonging at school. Others share how many of their antisocial behaviors decrease.

I remember a fifteen-year-old boy, who lived in a high-risk environment, sharing how, at the beginning of his mentoring relationship, he was on the fringes of a gang and had become involved in inappropriate behavior, taking days off school, while his academic performances had also declined.

He deliberately chose a policeman as his mentor. He felt he needed a firm, yet fair guide alongside him. Twelve months later he achieved distinctions in all his subjects, had chosen medicine as a career, and was free of antisocial behavior. His only regret was that he had been unable to encourage his negative peers to change their ways. I wonder what might have happened if all his peers had mentors alongside them?

Mentoring tip: An effective mentor is a rock their mentee can depend on, and a non-judgmental cheerleader.

DAY 2: EMPATHY AND THE WORLD

One of the great lessons I continually learn as a mentor of adolescents is linked to empathy. It is easy for me to forget how confused and lost I was at times during my adolescence—the many times of self-doubt; the times of feeling self-conscious; the occasions when I was too scared of failure to risk moving out of my comfort zone, and the stretches of loneliness when peer relationships floundered.

Sometimes it is important for mentors to step back from the busyness of life to reflect on their adolescent years before they meet up with their mentee. I work hard to acquire a deeper understanding of our global community—through the eyes of my mentee—fast-paced, and driven by technology.

Therefore, it is good to meet with my mentee and ask them how they feel about this global community. Their focus is most likely to be only on their local community. When they trust me, they become more open and willing to share honest feelings. I hear some excitement about what lies ahead as well as some fears about the unknown future, the potential disappearance of many of the current professions, and how they will use their gifts and talents to make a positive difference in the global community.

Continually sow messages of hope in these young lives.

Mentoring tip: Your mentees will better understand you as you share your values. Explain why these values are important, yet never impose them on your mentees.

DAY 3: MENTORING—A BONDING OF HEARTS

I always encourage mentors not to fall into the trap of comparing their relationship with their mentee with the experiences of other mentors.

Mentoring is "never" a competition.

Think about it. Every mentoring relationship has to be different because, for a start, we are all unique individuals with our own personal gifts and talents.

Two strangers from different backgrounds, with different fears, different interests, of different ages, and with different expectations of life, come together and embark on a journey together for a period of time.

The relationship will develop over time into a deeper friendship, as these two people connect with one another. They come to enjoy each other's company and the level of trust deepens.

The adolescent experiences unconditional care, and has an encourager and supporter walking alongside them, to guide them as they make decisions about the way ahead.

As the mentee feels safer and more secure in the company of their mentor, two hearts will bond—a magical, and special moment in two lives.

Mentoring tip: Effective mentors continually practice empathy, are authentic, and non-judgmental.

DAY 4: THE SIX SENSES OF RESILIENCY

The Institute for Mental Health Initiatives[1] at George Washington University highlighted these six senses of resiliency—which I have adapted for mentors—that can be nurtured during the mentoring journey. They reveal the outcomes of a relationship in which the mentor and mentee have a strong connection with each other.

1. *A sense of worth*: Resilient people feel loved and valued. They know that their contributions to family and extended family, school, work, and community can make a positive difference.

2. *A sense of hope and optimism*: Resilient people have dreams and goals for the future. They believe that things will turn out okay. For many, religious belief fuels this faith in the future.

3. *A sense of competence*: Resilient people know how to solve problems and communicate with others. They have concrete skills they can use to benefit themselves and others. They draw on their skills and sense of competence to manage adversity.

4. *A sense of goodness*: Resilient people are empathetic, and care. They act on their compassion. Their goodness prompts them to help others. Research states that this is one of the most effective ways to help oneself through times of stress.

5. *A sense of power*: Resilient people believe that they have the capacity to change their circumstances. They can take positive action to

---

1. Washington, *Competent Kids*.

overcome trauma, or change chronically debilitating circumstances with this sense of self-worth.

6. *A sense of community*: Resilient people recognize that they do not have to fix all their problems alone. They are part of a family, or an extended family, school, workplace, neighborhood, or faith community. These groups and communities can supply support, resources, and the political will that is sometimes necessary to bring about change.

Mentoring tip: Effective mentors, who reinforce whatever their mentees do that is strong, nurture resiliency.

MENTORING MOMENTS

Seventeen-year-old Emily found herself in trouble far too often. Indeed, many students and teachers felt she was fortunate to be allowed to remain at the school. Her quick temper, loud outbursts and disrespectful behavior resulted in her coming to speak to me in my office.

For the final eighteen months of her school career Emily slowly, but surely invited me into her life. We had many tough conversations, though we both had a great sense of humor, similar sport interests, and she knew that I could envision her achieve her career goal if she worked consistently. I advised her that I would not quit on her—it was tempting to do so at times.

Emily surprised her family and many teachers and friends when she gained an entrance to continue her studies at university. She graduated from university and moved into her dream career which involved helping people.

She handed me this treasured note on her final day at school, which reminded me for the umpteenth time of how important it is to remain a non-judgmental cheerleader who embraces the spirit of mentoring.

> Thank you for helping me get through school! I guess school just wasn't really my thing. I really appreciate all the time that you gave up to ensure I attended classes, got my work done, that I was on the right track with my life, and so much more! Thank you for inspiring me to be a better person! You gave me hope that I will still have a chance in life when I graduate with a score that reflects not even half my potential! I don't think I can express enough how grateful I am for everything you do for me! Even if I don't always show it! But most of all, thank you so much for never giving up on

me and always pushing me to achieve my best! You have made me a better person.

Mentoring tip: Patience, perseverance, and non-judgmental listening are key qualities to establish meaningful connections with youth.

Week 46

MENTORING QUALITIES REVISITED

> Don't be discouraged if your children reject your advice. Years later they will offer it to their own offspring.
> —Oscar Wilde

DAY 1: QUALITIES OF A MENTOR—A REFLECTION

It is good to reflect on what mentees have said about their mentors to help us understand what these young people need from us, as their non-judgmental cheerleaders.

You will hear a variety of comments. The one that I have heard the most is: "My mentor never quits on me!"

Here are some of the encouraging comments made by young people about their volunteer adult mentors and their mentoring experience in programs with which I have worked.

"I admired my mentor."

"We had fun together."

"She accepted me where I was."

"... a consistent, stable person in my life."

"A person of character, trustworthy."

"Affirming."

"We enjoyed a natural and positive relationship."

"He believed in me."

"He saw the potential in me which I could not see."

"She never seemed to judge me."

"I knew my mentor wasn't perfect, and that didn't matter."

"He saw me as a person of value."

"He cared for me."

"She let me go at my pace, and I really appreciated that."

"A helping hand when I was struggling."

"He was genuine."

Mentoring tip: Effective mentors are "always" supportive, flexible, caring, non-judgmental, and good listeners.

DAY 2: MENTORS MOVE OUT OF THEIR COMFORT ZONES

Mentors are special people who venture into the unknown during a time of confusion in a young person's life. Well-known psychologist Dr. Jay Giedd reminds us: "teens are navigating a cerebral hurricane without a compass."

In many ways, the mentor becomes the navigational compass in the young person's life for a period of time. The better you know yourself and the more people know about you, the more open and effective your communication and working relationship with your mentee.

One of your key functions as a mentor is to assist your mentee to apply what they are learning in school or the work place to everyday life. You can broaden their knowledge and provide opportunities to explore new situations, new places, and new cultures. You assist youth to translate their life experiences into learning opportunities. For example, if your mentee likes fixing things, you can talk about physics, electricity, and other sciences involved in careers which require these subjects. What careers are available? Maybe your mentee likes fashion—this allows you to talk about how designers use mathematics, while those in the marketing world study human behavior and use psychology to create advertisements or maximize the use of social media platforms.

The key challenge for both mentors and mentees is to move out of their comfort zones. Can you do this? Are you prepared to try?

A mentee is encouraged and empowered to enter more meaningful relationships with peers and other adults in the future, through forging a positive and meaningful relationship with a mentor.

Throughout the relationship demonstrate one of life's "Golden Rules": treat others the way you want to be treated—discuss the meaning of this with your mentee and how it applies to your respective lives.

Mentoring tip: Your mentee has special gifts and talents. Be flexible and accept this unique individual as you develop a meaningful mentoring relationship.

DAY 3: MENTORING ATTITUDES AND VALUES

I love the definition of a mentor shared by mentoring expert Bobb Biehl[1]: "Mentors are those who have gone before us on the mountain of life, but who pause and extend a hand to help us along the way, or who extend a safety line of love and affirmation that may keep us from falling off the mountain."

This reminds me how important it is to express an attitude of unconditional care towards the young people I mentor.

Sometimes they will struggle, perhaps fall over. However, because of my life experiences, I can reach out a helping hand and guide them along the next part of life's journey. As I do this, and look for opportunities to affirm and encourage them, remain non-judgmental, and display empathy, I model my values which, hopefully, inspire my mentees.

And, in the long-term, perhaps mentors will contribute to the establishment of a global mentoring community in which *everyone* feels loved, and cared for.

Mentoring tip: Effective mentors commit time to their mentees, have skills in a specific field, a sense of community service, are kind, concerned, and authentic.

DAY 4: THE MENTORING LEGACY

The non-judgmental mentor and cheerleader play a significant role in an adolescent's life.

Global mentoring expert Rey Carr[2] points out that, although the mentor may share similarities with teachers, counsellors and coaches, the mentoring relationship is unique, as it is neither a professional relationship, nor is it limited to only certain areas in a person's life.

1. Biehl, *Mentoring*, 26.
2. Carr, *Mentorship*.

Rey makes a critically important point:

> Mentoring is not a panacea. It alone cannot resolve the educational, family, social and labor issues associated with helping young people make a successful transition to the world of work. Mentoring must be integrated into a systematic and comprehensive strategy to improve the quality of life for all people. We can recruit people from all walks of life to be mentors. We can recognize that all youth will benefit from being in contact with healthy, responsible and skilled peers and mentors. We can add support to community volunteer programs in general. We can increase local community ownership of such volunteer activities. We can ensure that young people will make a successful transition from school to work today. If we do these things, we can increase the likelihood that the children of today's students will make successful transitions in a future world we cannot imagine today.

Mentoring tip: Allow your mentee to become part of your loving and caring world—what a privilege.

MENTORING MOMENTS

I have interacted with many people involved in youth mentoring over the years, and remain grateful for their willingness to share experiences, ideas, and resources.

I met Michael Garringer during my tour of more than twenty mentoring programs in Canada and America as part of my Churchill Fellowship a few years ago.

We remained in touch and exchanged information about resources we were developing. I informed Michael of my recent retirement, and received this humbling message.

> Thank you again for everything you did for the mentoring movement, not only in your part of the world, but also internationally. I certainly know you inspired my career. I hope you find even more ways to keep improving the world now that you are retired!

And, so emerged this book. Another great example of a peer mentoring relationship.

Mentoring tip: Strive to encourage others to imagine their futures. Guide, coach, navigate, and assist them shape, and evaluate the course of their lives.

Week 47

CHAMPION GOAL ACHIEVERS

When the world says, "Give up," Hope whispers, "Try it one more time."
—Author unknown

DAY 1: ACHIEVE STRETCHING GOALS

A challenge for mentors, as they encourage mentees to set goals and chase their dreams, often involves guiding these young people to step out of their comfort zones. I never cease to be amazed at the impact mentors have on their mentees when this happens.

Here are some examples of what I have observed.

- A mentee set up an exercise program with the help of their mentor.
- A mentee visited a computer firm with his mentor and learned how to rebuild computers before he set up his own small business from home.
- A mentee applied for a job and was rejected. This was a major setback for the mentee. Her mentor encouraged her to persevere. Six months later, with an improved attitude, she applied for a new job with the help of the mentor, and was employed.
- A mentee (like many others) built her goals around obtaining a driver license with the encouragement and support of her mentee.
- A mentee worked towards obtaining an overseas study scholarship. Her mentor helped her to prioritize, plan, and move out of her comfort zone to undergo new experiences so she would stand a better chance of obtaining the scholarship.

Mentoring tip: An effective mentor has the ability to see the bigger picture, and to speak to the potential the mentee may be unable to see for a variety of reasons.

DAY 2: A HOLISTIC GOAL SETTING PROCESS

I tend to look at a holistic approach, which focuses on the development of the "whole" person, when I embark on a goal setting journey with youth.

We look at goals that are related to education, physical fitness and health, social and cultural pursuits, family and home, and even incorporate spiritual and ethical matters in our discussions.

We are encouraged by more and more neuroscience research which, according to psychologists Richard Guare and Peg Dawson[1] states: ". . . the adolescent brain is primed for the acquisition of new skills. Teens are driven to seek out new experiences, more intense social and emotional relationships, and, for better or worse, new risks."

Psychologist Jennifer Fox Eades[2] reminds us that social support, a feeling of optimism, a sense of meaning, a focus on a mentee's strengths and goal setting, helps youth from difficult backgrounds (especially) to excel, and develop resilience.

Mentoring tip: Effective mentors encourage their mentees to stand on their own feet, become reliable and accountable, and trust them to achieve their goals.

DAY 3: A MENTOR: A CAREER EXAMPLE

A mentor shared an experience with his adolescent mentee. The young man was interested in fitness and was paired with this particular mentor who was a professional triathlete.

One afternoon they went on a training ride. The mentor chose a steep hill as part of the course they would ride. When he reached the top of the hill, he looked back, only to discover his mentee walking up the hill with his bike, too exhausted to ride. The mentor smiled and offered a word of encouragement.

Two weeks later, when the mentor met his mentee, the mentee shared that he could ride up that hill with no stops. What had happened in a subtle way was that a mentor had quietly laid down the challenge to his mentee to work at his fitness. The challenge had been accepted.

This modeling is an important aspect of the mentoring journey. The mentee had observed his mentor at work, compared himself with his

---

1. Guare and Dawson, *Smart but Scattered*.
2. Fox-Eades, *Celebrating Strengths*.

mentor, decided to emulate his mentor rather than quit, and so changed his attitude and behavior.

A growth mindset occurs in a young person's life as a mentor offers emotional support, and verbal feedback. New possibilities emerge, new horizons beckon, and the goal getting process heads in an exciting new direction, as occurred in this story.

Mentoring tip: An effective mentor sees solutions, as well as obstacles. Teach your mentee to be solutions focused.

DAY 4: CONSTRUCTIVE COMMUNICATION—GIVE FEEDBACK

Mentors are encouraged to continually work hard at constructive communication with their mentees. Feedback is one way to offer constructive assistance and to guide a young person during their journey of self-discovery. Here are some ideas.

- Prompt your mentees to consider a change to their behavior. For example, you provide feedback on how their behavior affects others.
- Keep your mentees on track. For example, you give feedback in relation to their goals.
- Coach your mentee how to live a healthy and balanced lifestyle. For example, you listen to your mentee describe their management of time, and discuss ways to improve, or have a better balance to their days.

Your mentees require honest, positive, and constructive feedback in order to improve. If they do not understand their strengths and developmental needs, how can they develop and learn?

Here are some tips I have used for many years, which make sure I offer constructive and genuine feedback.

- Do not give feedback until you have established the correct climate. This is a strong, trusting relationship. Your mentee feels safe and secure at all times.
- Provide a balance of positive and negative—and, if you need to criticize, comment on the *behavior* rather than the *person*—mentees are already receiving answers to questions they ask themselves, almost on

a daily basis: Who am I?; Why am I here?; Where am I going?; What is the meaning of this?; What is my purpose in life?

- Be specific and descriptive when you give feedback, and make sure the feedback is relevant.
- Provide feedback at an appropriate time. Ask your mentee if they would like feedback before you give it.
- Offer feedback that encourages further discussion.

Mentoring tip: Recognize and genuinely applaud your mentees' achievements—always as the non-judgmental cheerleader.

MENTORING MOMENTS

Sixteen-year-old Liam and I had a discussion when he was referred to me by a colleague. Liam's behavior caused concerns. Some of his peers felt he was a bully.

I asked Liam if he wanted my help. He responded positively to that question, and so began a two-year mentoring partnership. He struggled academically, and was passionate about sport.

Liam experienced many ups and downs, though he genuinely wanted to learn and improve his behavior. He also knew he had leadership qualities which needed nurturing. His academic results improved, and he surprised many of his critics when he was an outstanding captain of his first sport team during his final year of school.

I observed greater self-confidence, more self-discipline, significantly improved communication skills, and a calmer young man.

Liam wrote me this note on his final day at school.

> I want to thank you for taking the time out of your day to sit with me and get through these last couple of years. It undoubtedly shaped my attitudes and pushed me to succeed. Without you believing in me I would not have believed that I could ever have achieved what I have these past years.

Mentoring tip: Always genuinely value and respect the ideas and opinions of youth—you might be the only person in a young live doing so.

Week 48

MENTORS AND SIGNIFICANT ADULTS

The brain appears to undergo a growth spurt of its own; and this changing brain may in part explain why teenagers turn into a walking army of emotional loose cannons.

—Molly Edmondson

DAY 1: MENTORS ARE SIGNIFICANT ADULTS

Well-known clinical psychologist Tony Humphreys[1] stated:

> ... most children who are troubled and have learning difficulties within classrooms come from problematic home situations and have self-esteem difficulties. The resolution of conflicts within homes and the elevation of children's self-esteem are major responsibilities for parents and determine not only their children's educational development but also their emotional, social, and sexual development.

These findings make the mentoring journey a challenge. The wide range of influences on your mentee's self-worth include the self-esteem levels of both parents, how the parents relate to one another, and your mentee's experiences with other relatives. These relationships are the looking glass through which your mentee develops their self-esteem.

Sometimes mentors feel defeated and helpless by challenges mentees present during the mentoring journey.

---

1. Humphreys, *Self-esteem*.

However, be encouraged. I love this powerful statement by Tito, a former gang member—shared by researcher Lisa Delpit[2]: "Kids can walk around trouble, if there is some place to walk, and someone to walk with."

Lisa Delpit also shared an encouraging comment made by some youth who shared their thinking about the positive impact significant adults had in their lives: ". . . they held visions of us that we could not imagine for ourselves."

Mentoring tip: Great mentors model a positive approach to life and share messages of hope with their mentees.

DAY 2: A KEY STATEMENT IN LIFE'S JOURNEY

Here is a *key* sentence that defines who we are, and who we will become, which mentors can remember throughout the mentoring journey: What I *think* about myself affects how I *feel* about myself, and this determines how I *act*.

Expressed another way: our thoughts determine our feelings and help explain our actions.

Research has highlighted the important role parents play in the life of our youth.

- Each parent's own level of self-esteem influences that of a child.
- How parents relate to one another contributes to how secure or insecure a child feels.
- The development of a positive self-image and high self-esteem are important. These are the three key psychological tasks adolescents should accomplish.

    1. A sense of personal identity.
    2. Begin a process to establish relationships that are characterized by commitment, and intimacy.
    3. Begin to make decisions which lead towards training and entry into a particular occupation, or vocation.

The important and significant role of a mentor as the wise guide on the side facilitating this life journey is clear.

---

2. Delpit, *The Politics*.

Mentoring tip: Effective mentors are people lovers and unabashed lovers of life.

DAY 3: MENTEES WITH HIGH SELF-ESTEEM

Mentors nurture their mentees as these young people attempt to make sense of the confusion that typically abounds during adolescence. High self-esteem is essential for healthy living and the formation of meaningful relationships.

Here are some of the positive signs of mentees with high self-esteem, collated from many years of research:

- assertive behavior;
- good communication skills, which includes excellent listening skills—how to give feedback, ask for clarification, ask questions, restate opinions, or responses—and learning how to express themselves both verbally and in writing. Educator Dr. Paul Browning[3] writes:

  > When we truly listen, we are not just suspending our preconceptions about a situation or refraining from making a judgment, we are exposing ourselves to a particular vulnerability. We are putting at risk preconceptions of the world, our own beliefs, and our values.

- acceptable risk taking, which includes a risk as they move out of their comfort zone;
- responsibility for their own life choices, rather than blaming others for their feelings and problems; and an understanding of what it means to be accountable for their actions;
- a positive attitude (positive thinking);
- the ability to admit and deal with mistakes and life's disappointments, and a readiness to try something again even if they fail more than once;
- the courage to try something new or different;
- the ability to stick at tasks and clear goals until completion—rather than to quit when the going is tough—and to experience a feeling of comfort when they fulfill responsibilities;

---

3. Browning, *Principled*, 29.

- clarity about their beliefs and values so they can withstand negative peer pressure. This includes the ability to stand up for themselves and for their beliefs, sometimes to gain a sense of enjoyment because they are different.

Mentoring tip: Be a committed, steady presence in your mentee's life—reliable, consistent, trustworthy, and dependable.

DAY 4: DEVELOP A GREAT MENTORING RELATIONSHIP

Author Dorothy Briggs made the comment that it is the child's feeling about being loved or unloved that affects how they will develop. So, as a mentor of youth, what strategies can you pursue to make sure that your mentee feels loved and cared for?

Here are a few ideas to reflect upon during the mentoring journey from my personal mentoring experiences and extensive global research.

- Accept and appreciate your mentee as a young person, even though you may not accept their behavior. That is, provide unconditional love and care.
- Display empathy toward your mentee.
- Admire your mentee for *who* they are and respect privacy. Mutual respect fosters trust, and confidence.
- Be prepared to lead as you keep the lines of communication open, especially during times of conflict.
- Express trust in your mentee. You continually work to establish this trust—an important process to establish a two-way mentoring relationship.
- Remain willing to fearlessly reveal your own personality to your mentee. Sometimes your openness helps empathy—your mentee sees that you have "been there, done that," and learned from the experience.
- Be spontaneous and natural when you relate to your mentee.
- Have fun, and take pleasure in each other's company.

Mentoring tip: Mentoring involves making an emotional investment in a mentee's life: build trust, inspire and encourage, and make a positive impact.

MENTORING MOMENTS

Peter's life was tough. His parents were going through a messy divorce and he was struggling in all areas of his sixteen-year-old life.

I taught Peter and also coached him. He worked incredibly hard to develop his basic sport skills. He was a natural talent on the sport field and would eventually represent his country at the highest level.

My initial focus was to motivate and encourage Peter when I began meeting with him during this journey to find meaning and purpose. As he gained in confidence, he set new academic performance goals, and we discussed how to live a healthy and balanced lifestyle.

Peter's mother wrote me this humbling note.

> I would like to thank you from the bottom of my heart for all that you have done to help Peter since you have been at [the school]—not the least of which has been raising the money to enable him to go on the overseas sport tour. Peter has spoken often of the tremendous guidance and encouragement you give him and I know that your influence has strengthened and helped him through times when he has felt totally desperate about our home situation. It's people like you and so many others at [the school] that have given us both strength and made the nightmare of the past two-and-a-half years not quite so horrific.

Mentoring tip: As a non-judgmental cheerleader, always seek to recognize and applaud both the efforts and achievements of young people with whom you connect.

Week 49

MENTORING REFLECTIONS

When your passion and your intellect intersect you are unstoppable.
—Peter Legge

DAY 1: CHASE THE DREAM

Well-known boxer Sugar Ray Robinson described a dream as: "something that you feel so strongly about that you see yourself accomplishing it." A mentor has an important role to play as they guide and encourage their mentees to chase their dreams. I place a strong emphasis on this when I mentor youth.

Here are some proven strategies to consider.

- Share some of your goals with your mentee to show that the two of you are in a collaborative and developmental relationship. Share your dream or a story of how you achieved a dream, especially when you were a teenager.

- Encourage your mentee to develop a feeling of optimism about their future.

- Encourage an appreciation that your mentee wields great personal power as they have control over most of their choices. Mentees value your support as they develop the courage to act and to take risks that are not life-threatening.

- Encourage goals that are aligned with family or extended family values when you are involved in a cross-cultural mentoring relationship especially. An important question may be: "What is the attitude of your culture towards education and goal setting?" Wherever possible, the goals should be shared with the mentee's family or extended family.

Mentoring tip: An effective mentor is a guide, a teacher or coach, the keeper of selective wisdoms your mentee hopes to gain.

DAY 2: MY MENTOR

Youth mentoring expert Thomas W. Dortch Jr.[1] shares the words of an adolescent mentee which describe the great connection between the mentee and their volunteer adult mentor:

> It is an amazing feeling to have someone believe in you and help you pave the way. It makes everything seem possible. And I am so proud now when I speak to my mentor on the phone and tell him about the classes I am taking and everything I am doing. I feel like it's an opportunity to let him know that his trust and support are paying off. It is really important to me to have him proud of who I am becoming.

The role of an effective mentor is to encourage the growth of their mentee. Do your best not to come across as judgmental, most especially during the early days of the relationship when you try to build a connection.

Your mentee must feel your authenticity as they experiment with new ideas and strategies, when they stumble and fall, feel frustrated, and do not appear on the outside to enjoy a positive development process. Hang in there! Be the encourager and non-judgmental cheerleader. Listen carefully to your heartbeat. One well-chosen word or gesture could be the life-changer for a mentee.

Mentoring tip: As a mentor you will gain increased wisdom, character growth, a deeper understanding of youth issues, and greater empathy from the time you spend with your mentee.

DAY 3: MENTORS AND THE LITTLE VICTORIES

When mentees are asked why their mentors have become so significant in their lives, there will be some common answers, although most will stress that they appreciated someone in their lives who did not quit on them.

They share how much they have appreciated the mentors' emotional support, how their mentors were always available to listen, and allowed them to share more personal and sensitive issues. They valued how their mentors helped them set and achieve their own performance goals,

---

1. Dortch Jr., *The Miracles*, 120.

encouraged them to stretch their wings, and become engaged in a variety of activities.

Mentoring expert Mark Freedman[2] said: "Mentoring is mostly about small victories as subtle change." Continually look for those small moments when you can catch your mentee doing something good, and can genuinely affirm their "efforts." On many occasions those small moments allowed me to establish the connection with my mentee, after which they stepped up to a new level in the chase to achieve their dreams.

Mentoring tip: A great mentor understands that the attitude of your heart is more important and more obvious than anything you say in response.

DAY 4: AN AUTHENTIC FRIEND

A mentor becomes an authentic friend and role model to their mentee as the mentoring journey gains traction.

It is okay to allow your mentee to fail sometimes, as long as they are not involved in life-threatening behaviors or activities. You reach out a hand, help your mentee up, unpack the journey and lessons learnt, develop new strategies together, and encourage your mentee to move on positively.

If, however, you feel out of your depth and concerned about your mentee's health and wellbeing, seek help from more experienced people.

Your mentee, as I have found over the years, will trust your judgment most of the time, as you are a dependable person in their life, a rock, a consistent presence they value more than they often share. These experiences are all about your mentee's discovery about who they are, what life is all about, and which direction they choose to follow. Former British Prime Minister Benjamin Disraeli said: "The greatest good you can do for another is not just to share your riches, but reveal to him his own."

Mentoring tip: Don't try to impress your mentees, rather let them impress you.

MENTORING MOMENTS

I met seventeen-year old Alex when he had dropped out of school and had been drifting for a while. He was an angry young man who had dabbled in drugs, abused alcohol, and displayed other antisocial behavior traits. He had rejected outside help.

2. Freedman, *The Kindness*, 95.

I saw a young man who was lost, lacked self-belief, and trusted no-one. We met for coffee every few weeks for about nine months. Gradually he began to trust me and we began to unpack some of his issues. Small, achievable performance goals were set and achieved. He was considerably more capable than he realized.

Alex's life began to gain meaning and purpose.

His mother wrote me a note at the end of the year.

> I cannot thank you enough for the support and encouragement you have given to my family this year. Please accept a very heartfelt "thank you" from me, and on behalf of Alex who will probably say it in a couple of years. I have been amazed at the difference some one-on-one male to male time has made to Alex and how it has built his self-esteem. Boys really do need strong male role models, there's no doubt. We were very blessed that you were in a position to help us. Thanks again for your willingness, your time, and all those coffees. I can't "repay" or make it up to you.

This was the beginning of Alex's journey to discover his true potential. There were more rollercoaster rides before he finally began to settle down, and carve a positive future for himself—an interesting mentoring season, and a reminder that not all mentoring relationships might have long-term positive outcomes. Mentors sow the seeds. Mentees make life choices.

Mentoring tip: A trustworthy, significant adult in a youth's life is reliable, responsible, dependable, and authentic.

Week 50

INVEST IN A LIFE

What we need are more people who specialize in the impossible.
—THEODORE ROOSEVELT

DAY 1: MENTORING: INVEST IN A LIFE

I like the word "investing" when I think about a meaningful mentoring relationship with a mentee. I commit my time and energy to the relationship, and also my life experiences, my values, and whatever else is needed to create meaningful opportunities for my mentee to fulfill their potential.

Much depends on the nature of your relationship with your mentee. There might come a time when your mentee is brought into your family, and when you meet your mentee's family. When the latter occurs, continually remind yourself that you are the mentor of an adolescent, and are not there to rescue, save or fix families, or to mentor another family member. Keep a healthy perspective on the mentoring relationship, and invest your time in the life of that mentee only, which was your commitment. Your mentee wants you to stay focused on your relationship with them, and does *not* want you to become side-tracked by getting involved with other family members in any way.

Mentoring tip: Encourage your mentee not to put off until tomorrow what could be done today. Model what this means as you share your life experiences.

DAY 2: THE ROLE OF A MENTOR REVISITED

A mentor wears a variety of hats during the mentoring journey as a mentor, a wise guide, a coach, and friend to their mentee.

Here are some of the different roles a mentor undertakes during the mentoring journey to help you appreciate how these roles positively impact the lives of young people. A great opportunity for some reflection about your mentoring experience.

Be a *M*otivator:	As your mentee sets out to fulfill their potential, they develop a belief in their own self-worth, and acknowledge that they have control over things that happen to them most of the time.
Be an *E*mpowerer:	Reassure your mentee that they are valued and they matter. They will connect with you when they feel safe, liked, and respected. Have realistic, yet high expectations, and communicate these to your mentee. Your mentee will influence the people with whom they interact, such as, peers, siblings, and other family or extended family members.
Be a *N*avigator:	Be prepared to negotiate clear boundaries with your mentee so that they understand the consequences of their choices when they cross these boundaries.
Be a *T*eacher:	Encourage your mentee to develop or refine important life skills. These include how to set goals, effectively manage their time, resolve conflicts, appreciate the lasting importance of learning, and to have a sense of purpose.
Be *O*pen-minded and non-judgmental:	Accept your mentees as they are. Remain objective—able to look at all sides of an argument or situation as you encourage your mentee to interact positively with others and learn how to cope with new situations.
Be a *R*eflector:	Model the important activity to take time out to reflect. Teach your mentee how to review their situation; look for the positive and affirming opportunities; how to learn from mistakes and other life experiences.

Mentoring tip: Teach your mentees values like: *you can never lose by doing the right thing!*

DAY 3: SUPPORTIVE MENTORS

I always enjoy listening to mentees share their mentoring journey experiences. In many cases they share how they developed more self-confidence, feel more capable as a result of learning how to set their own goals, and believe that they have made a friend—their mentor—for life.

What actually happened was that the mentee had a significant adult volunteer their time to consistently turn up for meetings, and invest much of themselves in this mentoring relationship.

The mentors have been authentic nurturers—occasional navigators through challenging times—and cheerleaders of these young people. While they probably had some difficult conversations along the way, the mentee did not feel judged. Mentees acknowledged that, as their mentors kept turning up, they obviously cared about their mentees.

Often adolescents battle to express their thanks for all that the mentor contributes to their lives. I prepare mentors for this during their mentor training—a selfless attitude. Mentors see the growth that takes place in their mentees' lives. This is how mentees express their gratitude for the time and energy mentors invest in the relationship.

Mentoring tip: A positive mentoring relationship leads to improved communication and trust between your mentee and their family.

DAY 4: THOUGHTS ON SELF-ESTEEM

One of a mentor's tasks is to encourage the development of high self-esteem in their mentees, so these young people can cope with life's challenges.

Mental health expert Dr. John Arden[1] states that our attitude determines how we approach life. He highlights the importance of resilience, the ability to "maintain hope in the face of adversity that things will eventually get better, while doing what it takes to make those things happen."

The Kidshealth[2] website stated that healthy self-esteem is a child's armor against the challenges of the world. Mentees who feel good about themselves have an easier time handling conflicts and resisting negative pressures. They tend to smile more readily and enjoy life. These mentees are realistic and generally optimistic.

Authors John and Agnus Sturt[3] remind us: "Good self-esteem means being at peace with ourselves and with others. Because we accept and respect ourselves, we can treat others that way too. People with good self-esteem take responsibility for their own lives and personal growth, but they also have a desire to care for others. They feel both capable and lovable."

Mentoring tip: Great mentoring involves encouraging your mentee to think about the future, and to set realistic and achievable goals.

---

1. Arden, *Rewire*, 169.
2. Kidshealth.
3. Sturt, *Created for Love*.

MENTORING MOMENTS

Professor John Morris, or "Prof." as he was affectionately known, was chair of the Board and a past student of a school where I was the principal. He was a brilliant academic and businessman with an international reputation, and an authentic servant leader, as described by educator Dr. Paul Browning[4]:

> . . .if they are modeling true servant leadership, they become known as people who are compassionate, their values are reflected in their behaviors, and their response and actions are directed towards the people who genuinely need support.

"Prof." trusted me, and believed in a vision my colleagues and I had for the school. We lived through challenging times of transition in South Africa's history. Our school, a pioneering non-racial school, was at the cutting edge of education. And, that is where "Prof." wanted it to be—unafraid to lead change, challenge authorities when we needed to do so, and risk creative and innovative ideas.

"Prof." mentored me for almost five years. He fitted me into his busy schedule. He never stopped challenging me to move out of my comfort zone, and to make the tough decisions that were needed. He was insightful, caring, had a great sense of humor, and was a magnificent wise guide at my side.

We made a wonderful team and I cherish the hours and achievements under "Prof.'s" leadership. His resiliency and selflessness made him a significant role model and trusted friend at an important stage of my career.

Mentoring tip: Ask your mentee: "What are your priorities?" Then become the wise guide on the side as you offer encouragement and support.

---

4. Browning, *Principled*, 157.

Week 51

THE INSPIRED LEADER

Always live your life with one more dream to fulfill.
—Sara Henderson

DAY 1: THE INSPIRATIONAL MENTOR

Over the years I have mentored hundreds of adolescents. Some journeys have been quite amazing, and others considerably hard work as many obstacles were confronted.

The key, though, was to make a positive connection with these young people, always focusing on their whole development, otherwise referred to as using a holistic approach.

Goal setting became a fundamental part of every journey. Here are a few strategies I have either used myself, or encouraged other volunteer adult mentors to use, and which have had positive outcomes.

- Spend time clarifying goals or interests that your mentee pursues. Have your mentee write these goals down. You encourage them to take ownership of these goals.
- Encourage your mentee to record goals on a video clip to play back to themselves regularly as a form of self-motivation.
- Take an interest in your mentee's schoolwork. Ask to see books. Encourage your mentee to phone, email, or text you when they achieve a goal in a test, or project—or even if the grade is not as good as it might have been, yet there are clear, positive signs of improvement. Congratulate *effort* rather than performance.
- Offer to help your mentee put together a resume.
- "Always" be open and willing to learn from your mentee. Be teachable.

- If your mentee battles with a specific goal, and perhaps loses interest, show the importance of a flexible, fun approach to goal setting, and make the necessary changes.
- Continually remind yourself to focus on the development of the whole person when you discuss goal setting with your mentee.

Mentoring tip: Great mentors work quietly behind the scenes, seek no pay or glory, simply the satisfaction of knowing they have reached out to a young person.

DAY 2: THE MENTOR AS A CHEERLEADER

When mentors encourage and support mentees to set and achieve personal goals, their authentic, non-judgmental cheerleader's role is a significant aspect of the mentee's goal getting journey.

Here are some proven tips which I have used in a mentoring role for many years.

- Avoid teasing, nagging, and guilt trips. Always focus on the positive development of your mentee.
- Give genuine praise. Your mentee will respect your authenticity more than anything else.
- Look for ways to reward your mentee. Behavior and efforts that are rewarded will be repeated. They contribute to the growth of a positive mindset and the development of intrinsic motivation. Devise your own reward scheme—special certificates, text messages, notes, or special outings.
- Encourage your mentee to set goals around the school year—term by term, or semester by semester—or, if your mentee has a job, or is in training, every three months.
- Encourage your mentee to use creative ways to set goals. There is no one method that works for all. Let your mentee experiment and adapt. Develop the habit of writing their goals in a diary or journal. Maybe you could provide the journal. Allow for the uniqueness of your mentee.

Mentoring tip: Remind your mentees that when they think about what they do today, they influence the achievement of their dreams tomorrow.

DAY 3: TEN RULES OF EFFECTIVE LEADERSHIP

Some years back I did some work on leadership, and took the word *leadership* (ten letters) and wrote a quality or phrase linked to effective and selfless leadership alongside each letter. These qualities are relevant to the mentoring role, as a mentor is a leader or a person of positive influence.

> *L*ead by example at all times.
> *E*nthusiasm is contagious.
> *A*dmit my mistakes.
> *D*edication and commitment to the team.
> *E*nrich the lives of those I lead.
> *R*espect is earned, not a right.
> *S*piritual foundations change hearts.
> *H*umility, combined with a sense of humor.
> *I*ntegrity and loyalty go hand in hand.
> *P*ersevere in the face of adversity.
>
> I added three PET leadership qualities to this list:
>
> *P*atience.
> *E*mpathy.
> *T*olerance.
>
> I concluded with this statement: "To lead is to serve, and give of oneself expecting nothing in return."

Mentoring tip: All your mentee might need to know is that you are genuine, concerned, and caring—qualities no-one else might be displaying in that young life.

DAY 4: A TIME TO SHARE

As far as I am concerned, the *key* word in a mentoring journey is *relationship*.

Mentoring expert Rey Carr[1] stated: "A central purpose of any mentoring relationship is to allow both the volunteer and the mentee to share and explore with one another their perceptions of themselves, each other and their community."

Rey believes that too often the potential inherent in young people goes unrealized, or is under developed, when they do not have adults in their lives who care about them, and demonstrate that caring in practical, and supportive ways.

---

1. Carr, *Mentorship*.

When we work with young people from high risk environments, we can assist these mentees more effectively when the school and community expand their vision from one of being part of a community, to one of being "partners" in community. I have seen these positive partnerships work successfully in school-based youth mentoring programs especially.

Rey also stated: "Mentoring can provide for a context whereby, in building relationships with credible adult role models who are experiencing personally fulfilling and accessible life styles, young people from high-risk environments can conceive of the potential, perceive the route and create their own sense of relevance."

Mentoring tip: Create a nurturing environment in which your mentee discovers that failure is not fatal.

MENTORING MOMENTS

Alyson Groom was a retired school principal when I met her at a staff development day. In my role as a senior leader, the principal wanted me to have a supportive person I could speak to in confidence, and who was not linked to the school in any way.

Alyson lived in another country yet was always available when I wanted to chat. We arranged a mutually agreed time and then chatted for an hour.

Alyson was an exceptional listener, probably the best listener I have met. She clarified what I shared, helped me evaluate and unpack thoughts, and "never" judged me. Although we were separated by thousands of miles, her level of empathetic care continually astounded me.

After every conversation with Alyson I felt inspired and motivated. She helped me put some significant challenges in perspective, always made sure I felt safe and secure when we chatted, and, on more than one occasion, she spoke to my potential that I had struggled to see for a while.

I will always be indebted to Alyson for modeling the spirit of mentoring. A special person and a valued friend for a season.

Mentoring tip: Always remember your own childhood experiences when you empathetically confront youth.

Week 52

FINAL REFLECTIONS

Great things are done by people who think great thoughts and then go out into the world to make their dreams come true.

—Ernest Holmes

DAY 1: BUILD MEANINGFUL MENTORING RELATIONSHIPS

I wrote *Mentoring Journey* during a time of reflection about all my mentoring experiences.

> Confused, trying to unravel, understand
> life's intricate, pictureless puzzle
> through tinted, frustrated, alert eyes.
> Outwardly disinterested, sharp listener.
> Moody. Rainbow emotions: "Whaddaya know?!"
> Verbal protests mask insecure, fragile,
> awakening seeds of greatness.
> Bravado?! Adolescence!
> Persevere.
> Walk in their shoes.
> Occasional blistering, painful experiences
> threaten to derail envisioned images–
> golden, sun-filled days; dreamy sweat-stained
> mountain peaks triumphantly conquered.
> A stumble—curses, swears, mutters—
> potentially self-destructing, downward
> spiral rears a tortured head.
> Respectfully reach out, take a hand;
> smiling, wise eyes, whisper softly, sincerely:
> "I believe in you!"
> The nurturing journey continues.

FINAL REFLECTIONS

Mentoring tip: There are no quick-fix solutions to develop a positive mentoring relationship. It is a process that takes time.

DAY 2: JUSTIFY YOUTH MENTORING GLOBALLY

Youth mentoring programs in which volunteer adult mentors assist young people to make sense of confusion in their lives are justified by numerous youth-related issues.

Such issues, supported by years of research, include the need to deal with:

- negative peer pressure
- truancy
- cigarette smoking, or vaping
- social and time management
- career exploration, and part-time work
- exploration of faith and religion
- gender issues
- irresponsible use of social media
- anxiety
- child abuse, and family or extended family violence.
- alcohol and drug abuse
- youth suicide
- use or abuse of social media
- depression

Young people who do not participate in work, education, or training, may be described as inactive, disengaged, or disconnected. Those who are inactive for lengthy periods of time have a highlighted risk of poor outcomes, which might include any of the following common examples:

- lower earnings
- criminal offending
- suicide
- higher rates of unemployment
- greater reliance on government social or welfare assistance
- substance abuse
- teenage pregnancy
- homelessness
- mental illness

Parenting behavior contributes significantly to a young person's self-esteem—non-compliance and antisocial behavior are related to low self-esteem.

In many cases, which involve youth from high-risk environments, a carefully developed mentoring program developed by professionals in a variety of youth-related fields would be needed.

Mentoring tip: Your mentee must feel safe and secure in your presence, always cared for, and often challenged in a positive, and encouraging way.

DAY 3: GO TO THE EDGE

Poet Guillaume Appollinaire wrote:

> "Come to the edge," he said.
> The people answered, "We are afraid."
> "Come to the edge," he said.
> They came.
> He pushed them.
> And they flew.

In many ways this is what mentoring adolescents is like for many mentors.

Imagine how you would feel if you came to the edge and faced the unknown. Behind you is everything you know and are familiar with, including your comforts. Ahead of you is the darkness or the unknown. Will you go over the edge and fall an unknown distance? Or will you trust the person by your side to coach and mentor you so you can fly high and discover new things about yourself and the world?

When you stand on the edge with your mentee allow them to take the next step at their own pace. Show understanding, have patience, and be the authentic cheerleader—a positively significant adult in that young life.

Baseball legend Jackie Robinson said, "A life isn't significant except for its impact on other lives."

Mentoring tip: An effective mentor is approachable, flexible, teachable, and open-minded.

DAY 4: MENTORING: A RELAY RACE

I often describe mentoring as similar to the experience of travelling on a road towards a bridge. The mentee walks across the bridge a little tentatively, perhaps, reaches the other side, looks back only to see that the bridge has collapsed, and there is no way back. A forward-looking journey is the only choice available.

And I, the mentor, stand, with a broad smile on my face on the other side of that bridge, and wave at my mentee, who understands my final message to them—because we have prepared for this moment: "Go and chase your dreams. You can do it! I believe in you! Stay in touch if you wish to." There are a variety of ways we can stay in touch: an email, a text message, or a phone call.

Imagine that, as the mentee parts company with me, I pass them a baton which I ask them to pass on to someone else at an appropriate time. Written on the baton are the words familiar to our relationship: "Be a goal getter. Stay humble. Celebrate the small achievements. Use my diary. Manage my time well. Be organized, and plan well. Laugh lots. There is only one unique me with my strengths, gifts and talents—give to others. Be a positive person of influence."

I hope that one day my mentee becomes a mentor, and life's relay race will continue from one generation to the next.

Mentoring tip: Great mentors encourage their mentees not to put off until tomorrow what can be done today.

MENTORING MOMENTS

We mentor adolescents and often have no idea how much impact we have on their lives. However, it remains an enriching and fascinating experience for both the mentors and the mentees.

Here are some comments written by volunteer adult mentors of fifteen-year-old students, most of whom were from low socio-economic areas. They attended a nine-month school-based program, for which students voluntarily applied.

> "Through the many activities and discussions we have shared, I have seen a development in his confidence, resilience, self-esteem and self-assurance. He is developing a strength to manage his behavior, his time, his skills and abilities. He is beginning to vision, dream and realize his brilliant potential! Has been a privilege to be a small part of this. An outstanding program—with amazing potential for many young people—and mentors too."

> "We worked through career and goal setting—thinking about people, life and jobs and did role plays and discussed experiences (real and possibilities)."

"His manner came across more confident and positive. He has become very open in conversation with me. Watching him go from so lazy and unmotivated, to become keen to get an apprenticeship and also seeing him looking forward to us meeting each week."

"I saw him grow in confidence and self-belief. All the "I don't know" and "it depends" answers diminished in frequency. There was also a change in his physical appearance—no longer hid behind long hair and he carried himself more confidently. He was always keen to meet together. At times when the going got a bit tough there was always good advice and encouragement. Feedback on how we were making progress was great . . . discovering career paths—his excitement and motivation when he realized what he wanted to do."

Mentoring tip: Always strive to model the attitudes you would like youth with whom you connect to have.

CONCLUDING THOUGHTS

Mentoring is servanthood, setting an example, combined with loving persuasion. The mentor appeals to the heart and mind of the mentee; sets an example by the way they live and move; serves the mentee with their gift and their life and, in so doing, wins the mentee's love and respect. The mentee follows the mentor because they wish to do so.

—Ron Boehme

I hope that these Mentoring Minutes messages have encouraged you as you journey alongside a young person, and continually reminded you of the power of face to face relationships.

The spirit of mentoring can embrace all our relationships as we learn how to be authentic, selfless, non-judgmental, and more empathetic, while we remain kind and patient with ourselves.

We have been reminded of the challenges involved in mentoring young people, pertinently summed up by mentoring expert Dr. Susan Weinberger[1]:

> The mentors and mentees should be regarded as the customers of mentoring programs, and information should be collected

---

1. Weinberger, *Developing a Mentoring program*, 230–231.

FINAL REFLECTIONS

from them regularly to determine how well the program is accomplishing its goals. Staff also should be helping to anticipate problems that might arise and to respond quickly to these issues and concerns. Even in the best of mentoring relationships, there will be times when mentors in particular, experience frustration, exasperation, impatience, anger, and even regret that they entered in the relationship in the first place.

I have shared true stories of my life journey which has been guided by remarkable mentors in specific seasons. These are my role models who have modeled the spirit of mentoring to me, and coached me to become a more competent, and confident mentor.

Pause. How many mentoring qualities can you observe in the following comments? There is no need to share the stories behind the comments to appreciate the sentiments being expressed.

> Thank you for the time that you have spent with me this year. I have certainly experienced significant personal and professional growth. But most of all I would like to thank you for the support you have given me through an extremely tough period in my life. Your care and kindness provided comfort and strength for me ... You have definitely "added value" to my life and I am grateful. (Abby)

> I am very grateful for all that you have done to help me on the field, in the classroom and otherwise. My folks realize what a great help you have been and are very grateful that someone like you was nearby to give assistance. Thank you for all you have done to help me as a teacher and as a friend. You have helped me to make the right decision about my education. (Daniel)

> This has been an unbelievably tough year both physically and emotionally but you have been my rock. Your patience and wisdom have allowed me to come to terms with my situation and start to look ahead to a more positive future. Your efforts have enabled me to grow and develop as a person and leader. Your offer to journey alongside me has allowed me to take risks and deal with the outcomes and for this I am eternally grateful. (Charlotte)

Phoebe was in her early twenties when she sent this message to me and three other colleagues. Many young adults who have been mentored during their adolescence would probably identify with Phoebe's experience.

Today, six years ago, I walked my slight, anxious and petrified self out of my high school and into a wide and open world. It's been an incredible journey so far, with beautiful highs and the occasional tremendous low. I'm incredibly grateful for the gift that was my time at school. I've been inspired to keep giving when I feel like I have nothing left in me, and to carry a spirit of respect and learning with me everywhere I go. We were built to be tough, confident, resilient and kind, with a generous spirit. I could never have asked for more. Thank you so much. Your influence on who I am is never going to be forgotten.

Mentors, peer mentors and mentees have shared thoughts and experiences against the backdrop of a variety of mentoring scenarios, an opportunity to celebrate all the amazing mentors who have invested their time and energy in the lives of others and, most especially, our youth. Yet there is more work to be done to encourage, guide, and support our youth to reach their potential. Over twenty-five years ago mentoring expert Marc Freedman[2] wrote:

> Through numerous pragmatic suggestions, a growing number of policymakers, researchers, and practitioners have recognized the need to 'build into our schools and other institutions that deal with young people a quality of caring, a friendly climate that makes them feel wanted, appreciated, and valued as individuals.'

Let these words of Ralph Waldo Emerson, which have hung by my desk throughout my career and which have continued to motivate me to be a positive person of influence in my community, inspire and challenge you: "Do not follow where the path may lead. Go, instead, where there is no path and leave a trail."

Youth mentoring has been the significant focus of this book, so it is apt to finish with a powerful message from fifteen-year-old Marion, who read this poem to her mentor Emma at the conclusion of the GR8 Mates school-based mentoring program I facilitated in Australia.

Friendship

You're my friend and that is true.
But the gift was from me to you.
We went through moments that were good and bad
Even moments that were happy and sad.
You supported me when I was in tears,

---

2. Freedman, *The Kindness*, 116.

FINAL REFLECTIONS

We'll stick together for years and years.

It's really sad that it has to be this way
But it has reached its very last day.
Miles away can't keep us apart,
Because *you* will always be in my heart.

ACKNOWLEDGMENTS

This book is the culmination of approximately forty-five years as an educator, sport coach, mentor, and youth mentor program developer. I have gathered quotes, notes from conferences, "gold nuggets" of wisdom and helpful tips from a variety of books, magazines, blogs, DVDs, websites, and general conversations with people.

The content of this book, therefore, is a tribute to the many people from a variety of backgrounds and professions who have shared their life experiences and wisdom either with me personally, or with the global community. Many of these people have generously shared their resources with me. Rey Carr is one such person who has always allowed me to quote his work freely. Rey's contribution to the global mentoring community over many years has been significant. I had the privilege of meeting him in Canada during my Churchill Fellowship travels.

Special thanks to mentoring expert Dr. Susan Weinberger who kindly wrote the Foreword to this book. Susan has generously shared resources and expertise with me on a number of occasions, most especially when I set up a school-based mentoring program, and I have always valued her insights, wisdom and mentoring expertise.

MENTOR (The National Mentoring Partnership) willingly shared resources and offered me advice and direction during my early years of involvement with youth mentoring program development, and remain at the forefront of the development of youth mentoring policies and other youth-related resources.

The research and writing of psychologist Professor Jean Rhodes have significantly influenced my thinking. I am grateful for her willingness to share ideas, opinions and research, and highly recommend *The Chronicle of Evidence-Based Mentoring*, one of the best sources for summaries of mentoring and research practice—www.evidencebasedmentoring.org

Ann Dunphy, Jim Peters, and Bill Gavin pioneered the establishment of the New Zealand Youth Mentoring Network. It was a privilege to assist them where I could, and to count them as valued friends and mentoring colleagues.

Nan Henderson's work on resiliency had a significant impact on my thinking after I attended one of her workshops in 1999, and I thank her for her willingness to share her resources.

Search Institute has willingly shared resources and expertise with me over many years, and I valued my visit to their office during my Churchill Fellowship travels. Their evidence-based research, the focus on developmental assets, and the work they do exploring the development of positive relationships contributes significantly to my thinking.

Ian Palmer CEO of the Schools Industry Partnership in New South Wales, Australia, is a visionary with a passion and the courage to explore innovative ways to inspire young people to reach their potential. I sincerely thank him for encouraging the successful trial of the GR8 Mates youth mentoring program in three schools in the area, which proved the power of school-based mentoring programs.

The Bibliography does not do justice to the resources I have used while writing this book. There is an extensive list of resources on my website www.yess.co.nz to give readers additional references for the content. If I have inadvertently failed to acknowledge a source, I would be most grateful if the reader would inform me of this so that I can rectify the omission before any further printings of this book.

Sincere thanks to Matthew Wimer and the editors of Resource Publications of Wipf and Stock for all their support, help and guidance—an incredible team.

Finally, this book would not have been possible without the encouragement and support of my wife Jane. She has always been my greatest critic and cheerleader, and also sacrificed many hours to help edit this book, for which I am *most* grateful.

BIBLIOGRAPHY

Arden John B. *Rewiring Your Brain: Think Your Way To A Better Life*. Wiley. 2010.
Barrett Beth, Annis Alan, Riffey Dennis. *Little moments Big Magic: Inspirational stories of Big Brothers and Big Sisters and the Magic They Create*. Magical Moments. 2004.
Barnard Peter A. *Socially Collaborative Schools: The Heretics Guide to Mixed-Age Tutor Groups, System Design, and the Goal of Goodness*. Rowan & Littlefield. 2018.
Benard Bonnie. *Fostering Resiliency in Kids. Protective factors in the family, school and community*. 1991.
Biddulph Steve. *Raising Boys*. Finch. 1997.
Biehl Bobb. *Mentoring: Confidence in finding a mentor and becoming one*. Broadman and Holman. 1996.
Bobrow Edwin E. *My Say: A mentor's guide to success*. Chandler House. 1999.
Browning Paul Dr. *Principled: 10 leadership practices for building trust*. University of Queensland Press. 2020.
Buckingham Jennifer. *Boy troubles: understanding rising suicide, rising crime and educational failure*. Center for Independent Studies. 2000.
Carr Rey. *Mentoring: The Bridging Model*. Peer Resources. 1997.
Cox Robin. *The Spirit of Mentoring: A manual for adult volunteers*. Essential Resources. 2017.
Delpit Lisa. 'The Politics of Teaching Literate Discourse'—in *City Kids, City Teachers: Reports from the front line*. Ayers W. and Ford P. (eds). New Press. 1996.
Dortch Jr. Thomas W. *The Miracles of Mentoring*. Broadway. 2000.
Feinstein Sheryl G. *Secrets of the Teenage Brain: research-based strategies for Reaching and Teaching Today's Adolescents (Second Edition)*. Corwin. 2009.
Fox Eades Jennifer M. *Celebrating Strengths: Building Strength-based Schools*. CAPP. 2008.
Freedman Marc. *The Kindness of Strangers: Adult Mentors, Urban Youth, and the New Volunteerism*. Cambridge University Press. 1993.
Fuller Andrew. *Raising Real People*. ACER. 2000.
Grant Ian. *Fathers Who Dare Win*. Pa's. 1999.
Grant Ian and Cowan John. *Parenting teenagers in the 1990s: The white-water rafting years*. Pa's. 1997.
Guare Richard, Dawson Peg, Guare Colin. *Smart but Scattered Teens: The "Executive Skills" Program for Helping Teens Reach Their Potential*. Guildford. 2013.
Henderson Nan, Benard Bonnie, Sharp-Light Nancy (eds). *Resiliency in Action: Practical ideas for overcoming risks and building strengths in youth, young families and communities*. Resiliency in Action. 2007.
Henderson Nan and Milstein Mike. *Resiliency in Schools: Making it happen for students and educators*. Corwin. 1996.
Humphreys Tony. *Self-Esteem: The key to your child's future*. Gill & MacMillan. 1996.

Institute for Mental Health Initiatives. *Competent Kids: A guide for fostering resilience.* George Washington University. Not dated.
Jensen Frances and Nutt Amy. *The Teenage Brain: A Neuroscientist's Survival to Raising Adolescents and Young Adults.* Harper. 2016.
Jucovy Linda. *Same-race and Cross-race Matching.* Public/Private Ventures. 2002.
Kidshealth website: https://www.kidshealth.org.nz
Lewis David. *One-Minute Stress Management.* Vermilion.1993.
Lindenfield Gael. *Success from Setbacks.* Thorsons. 1999.
Long Anne. *Listening.* Darton, Longman & Todd. 1990.
Manning Jessica. Article in *New Zealand Herald.* 11 April 2001.
Newman Tony. *Promoting Resilience: A Review of effective strategies for child care services.* Center for Evidence Based Social Services, University of Exeter. 2002.
Pekel Kent. *Moving Beyond Relationships Matter: An Overview of One Organizations Work in Progress.* Journal of Youth Development. Vol.14. Issue 4. University of Pittsburg. 2019.
Probst Kristie. *Mentoring for Meaningful Results: Asset-Building Tips, Tools and Activities.* Search Institute. 2006.
Rhodes Jean. *Four takeaways from a forthcoming book on youth mentoring.* Sourced from: *The Chronicle of Evidence-Based Mentoring*—www.evidencebasedmentoring.org. August 21, 2019.
Rhodes Jean and Christensen Kirsten. *Want to double your efforts? Hopefulness from a new meta-analysis.* Sourced from: *The Chronicle of Evidence-Based Mentoring*—www.evidencebasedmentoring.org. April 15, 2020.
Rhodes Jean E. *Stand by Me: The risks and rewards of mentoring today's youth.* Harvard College. 2002.
Siegel Daniel J. MD. *Brainstorm: An Inside-Out Guide to the Emerging Adolescent Mind, Ages 12–24.* Scribe. 2014.
Sinetar Marsha. *The Mentor's Spirit.* St. Martin's Griffin. 1998.
St Clair Barry and Carol. *Ignite the Fire.* Chariot Victor. 1999.
Stoddard David A. *The Heart of Mentoring: Ten proven principles for developing people to their fullest potential.* Navpress.2003.
Sturt John and Agnes. *Created for Love: Understanding and building self-esteem.* Guildford. 1994.
United States Education Department. *Yes You Can: A guide for establishing mentor programs to prepare youth for College.* United States Education Department. 1998.
Weinberger Susan G. *Preparing my Mentor for Me.* Governor's Prevention Partnership, CT. 2007.
Weinberger Susan G. and Forbush Janet B. *The Role of Mentoring in Chronic Absenteeism.* Kappan *BACKTALK.* March 2018.
Weinberger Susan G. (2005). *Developing a Mentoring Program (220–234).* In DuBois David L. & Karcher Michael J. (eds.). *Handbook of Youth Mentoring.* Thousand Oaks, CA: Sage Publications. 2013.
Wetmore Donald. *KISS Guide to Organizing Your Life (Keep It Simple Series).* DK. 2001.
Wooden John with Steve Jamison. *Wooden: A Lifetime of Observations and reflections On and Off the Court.* McGraw Hill. 1997.

www.ingramcontent.com/pod-product-compliance
Lightning Source LLC
Chambersburg PA
CBHW070243230426
43664CB00014B/2399